TERRY J. GANDER

TANKS & ARMOUR

PzKpfw I & II

TERRY J. GANDER

Acknowledgements
This book could not have been produced without the invaluable assistance of the following people: David Fletcher, Historian at the Tank Museum *(TM)*, Bovington, Dorset, England, and the Librarian Janice Tate; my gratitude to Thomas Anderson *(TAn)* for access to his wonderful collection of World War Two images; to the Axwall Museum, Sweden *(AxM)* and John Blackman *(JBn)*; finally to Mark Franklin for his excellent colour artworks.

John Prigent
August 2005

Series Created by Jasper Spencer-Smith.
Design: Nigel Pell.
Military Editor: John Prigent *(JP)*.
Produced by JSS Publishing Limited, PO. Box 6031, Bournemouth, Dorset, BH1 9AT, England.

TITLE SPREAD: A troop of PzKpfw Is on manoeuvres in the 1930s. *(TAn)*

ABOVE: A *Marder II* with the 7.5cm PaK 39 built on the PzKpfw II Ausf A, B, C and F chassis. *(TAn)*

COVER: A PzKpfw I on parade in the 1930s. *(TAn)*

First published 2006

ISBN (10) 0 7110 3090 1
ISBN (13) 978 0 7110 3090 9

Published by Ian Allan Publishing

an imprint of Ian Allan Publishing Ltd, Hersham, Surrey KT12 4RG
Printed in England by Ian Allan Printing Ltd, Hersham, Surrey KT12 4RG

0602/B3

Contents

Chapter 1

Development

To the casual observer the term Panzer still gives rise to images of armoured might and invulnerable tanks crushing the hapless opposition by speed, weight and firepower.

During the heyday of the *Blitzkrieg* up to 1940 many of the vehicles deployed were lightly armoured machine-gun tanks quite unfit to face enemy armour or anti-tank guns. The *Blitzkrieg* campaigns of 1939 and 1940 were largely carried out by the little PzKpfw I and the only slightly larger PzKpfw II, the modest forerunners of what were to become Germany's spearhead land weapon, the Panzer divisions.

Beginnings

Following the 1919 Treaty of Versailles the once mighty German Army was whittled down to the *Reichswehr*, an internal security force limited to 100,000 personnel and a restricted number of weapons. No tanks were allowed. Within this attenuated force the bulk of the manpower, officers and other ranks, were combat-experienced veterans of the Great War years who were determined to somehow reverse the strictures of the Versailles Treaty. Such a reversal of fortune would take time, new equipment and money.

But the 1920s were years of economic and social troubles for Germany so all the soldiers could aspire to was training to act as cadres of the army to come. The terms of the resented Treaty were supervised and enforced with some vigour during the early years of the decade, yet somehow the officers who formed a 'shadow' General Staff (a department specifically proscribed by the Treaty) obtained clandestine funds for in-depth research into the Great War campaigns. The results were not just historical. They were also analysed to determine future strategies and tactics, examine what form the future German armed forces should take, and establish how they would be organised, led and equipped.

In the midst of all this underground activity came examination of the potential of the tank, one of the few really new weapons of the Great War period. Despite subsequent events, the *Reichswehr* planners were at first lukewarm towards the tank, rating it as nothing more than an infantry support vehicle. Few serving officers had much experience of using tanks in battle and those few were unwilling to expand

ABOVE: The test vehicle produced as the La.s 100 (MAN). This type of suspension was fitted to the PzKpfw II Ausf b, but was not very successful and only used on a small production batch. *(AN)*

their ideas beyond crossing obstacles, rather than look towards the tank's mobile warfare potential. If the tanks/the war had continued into 1919 all manner of ambitious tank tactics had been forecast, but they never materialised and the few career soldiers still in uniform after 1919 settled back into their pre-1914 ways.

Despite all the apathy towards armoured vehicles, some tank-based innovations were studied in Germany. Somehow, money was found to fund a programme to build and learn more about tanks. This was particularly important for the *Reichswehr* as the old German Army was slow regarding tank development – few German-produced tanks ever reached the front lines during World War One. During the 1920s German industry was quietly encouraged to undertake tank design and development while at the same time a testing area was hired deep within the Soviet Union where tanks (and many other new weapons) could be evaluated far from the eyes of Treaty observers.

For the purposes of this account there is no need to delve into the details of these early experimental German tanks. Industrial and army personnel soon learned that there was more to tank development than manufacturing what looked good on a drawing board. The trial models proved to be unreliable while some of the more unfortunate aspects of contemporary tanks under development elsewhere were incorporated into the German designs.

The two main vehicles that emerged from this 'underground' period were deliberately mislabelled as *Traktor* (tractor) to disguise their true nature to Treaty observers - there were *leichte* (light) and *schwere* (heavy) examples. Their main contribution to the German tank programme was that they gave an insight into tank construction and technology while the finished vehicles gave tank personnel an indication of what they might need, plus experience in the employment of the tanks still to come.

New Ideas

One main shortcoming of these early inter-war German tanks was that they were developed without a true idea of what they were meant to

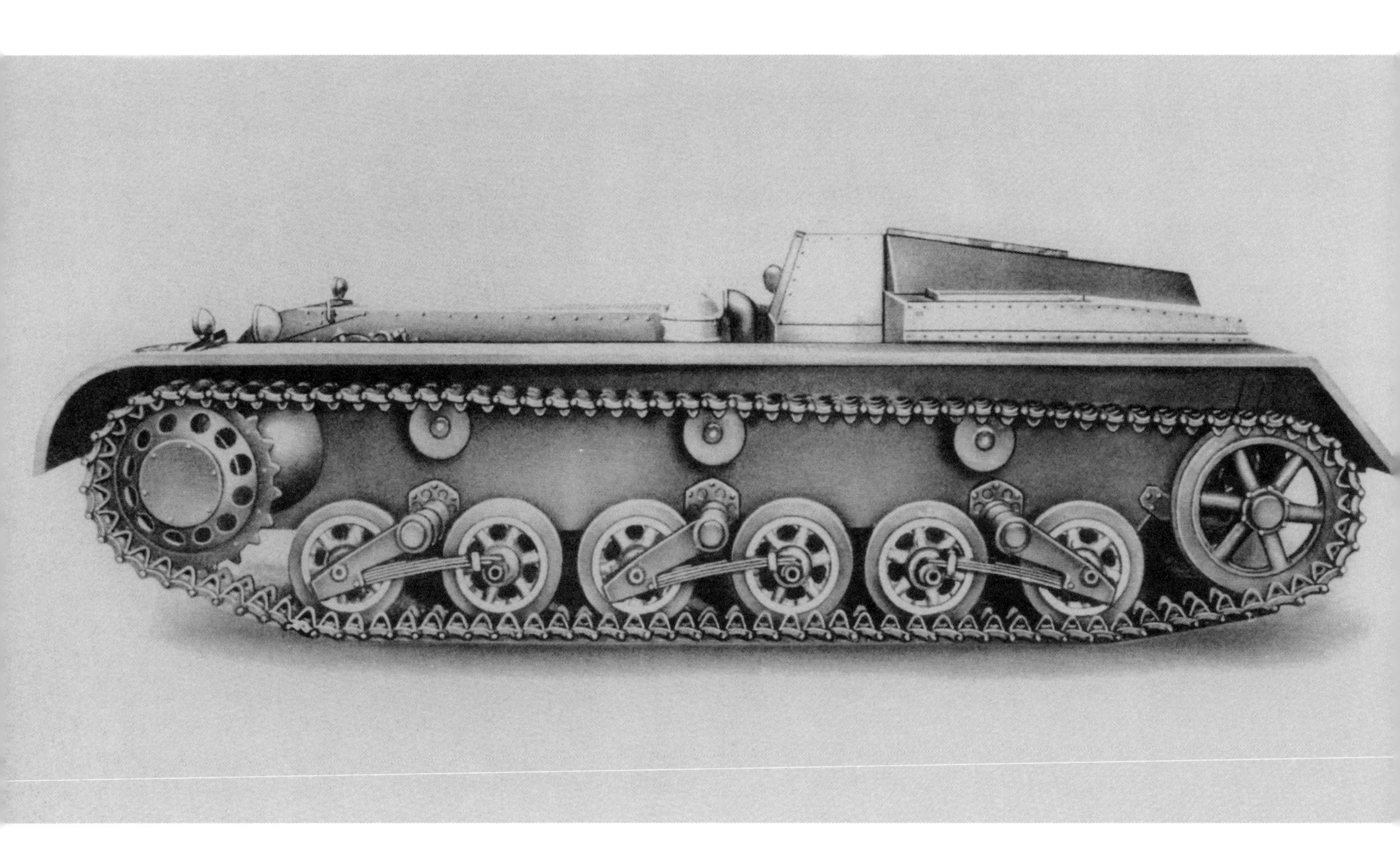

ABOVE: Competing designs were requested from several firms for a tank in the 10-ton class that was to become the PzKpfw II. This is the unsuccessful La.S 100 vehicle designed by Henschel. *(AN)*

do. As far as many involved in the programme were concerned the accepted infantry support function prevailed, but by the early 1930s new tactical ideas were attracting consideration. Instead of the mobile gun platforms of the 1920s, with their multiple turrets and ponderous performances, it was forecast that the future would lie with an entirely different type of tank with a better all-round automotive performance, a powerful armament and viable armoured protection, the overall emphasis being on speed and striking power.

It was here that the German historical analysis during the 1920s started to bear fruit. What emerged was that the *Sturmtruppen* break-through operations of 1918 were successful due mainly to their combination of shock tactics, deep infiltration and flanking movements, and highly organised yet flexible firepower. The one drawback was that progress was restricted by the physical limitations of the foot soldier. Once those limits had been reached, *Sturmtruppen* operations ground to a halt. The proposed solution was to utilise armoured vehicles in place of manpower alone.

Two enthusiasts stood out in Germany regarding these innovative ideas. One was General Lutz, Inspector of Motorised Troops, and the other Lieutenant-Colonel Heinz Guderian, his Chief of Staff. Of the two, Guderian was to have the most important long-term influence on armoured warfare for he not only proposed the formation of Panzer divisions but he also set out his ideas on paper to influence a larger audience than just his uniformed colleagues. He was but one of a handful of inter-war prophets of mobile armoured warfare who, throughout the 1920s, attempted to stimulate the acceptance of armoured warfare, although Guderian was the one to impose the greatest long-term influence.

Guderian envisaged a balanced and independently operating Panzer force of mechanised vehicles within which the tanks would be the main striking element, supported by mechanised infantry and combat engineers, reconnaissance units, self-propelled artillery, mobile signals, and so on. Aircraft would supply the heavy artillery effects. Such a force had already been formed on an experimental basis in the United Kingdom during 1927 and 1928. Unfortunately, not only did this experimental force fade away but many misleading conclusions were drawn from the results. This led to the

ABOVE: One of the pre-production PzKpfw I Ausf A vehicles built by Krupp in mid-1933. These were known as the 0-series and used for extensive testing. Here it is without the simple scoops used to direct air to the intake cleaners before the armoured superstructure had been built. *(AN)*

formation of an 'all-tank' force theory that prevailed for some years. Others, including the German observers who witnessed the experimental forces activities, tended to concentrate their thoughts on inter-arm cooperation and support.

During the early 1930s it was all too obvious that the formation of a viable *Panzer* force would take time, resources and money. These were commodities in short supply at that time but once Hitler's NSDAP came to power the situation changed dramatically. Guderian's ideas appealed to Hitler who bestowed his approval and made available the means to build the *Panzer* divisions.

Guderian foresaw that as far as tanks were concerned, no existing German vehicles could meet his specifications. Two main types would be required. One, the supposed main combat vehicle armed with a 50mm armoured-piercing gun, eventually emerged as the PzKpfw III (but at first armed with a 37mm gun. The second vehicle, with a short 75mm gun, was meant to provide high-explosive shell support and act as a breakthrough tank. It ultimately became the PzKpfw IV.

In 1933 both vehicles were still paper designs and nothing serviceable could reach the troops for several years to come. Design and development work on both vehicles was initiated but in the interim a relatively light and inexpensive training tank was required to familiarise all those involved, military and industrial, with the production of armoured vehicles and the operational challenges involving armoured forces, starting with the basics of driving and maintenance.

It was considered that the training requirement could be met by a simple design weighing approximately 5 tons (5,080kg) and carrying an armament of two machine guns. This became the *PanzerKampfwagen I* (PzKpfw I), entering production during 1933. By then it was apparent that the development of the two combat tanks was going to take even longer than had been anticipated so a slightly larger light tank armed with a 20mm cannon could act as a follow-on for the PzKpfw I in the training and familiarisation roles and perhaps act as a light reconnaissance vehicle should combat arise. This requirement resulted in the *PanzerKampfwagen II* (PzKpfw II) of 1935. For the non-technically minded, both vehicles also had the advantage of looking good on parade thereby adding to the impression of Germany's expanding military might.

ABOVE: The Krupp LKB3, converted from a PzKpfw I Ausf A in 1937 by installing a Krupp air-cooled engine and longer suspension. It was intended as a driver instruction vehicle for Sweden. Note the grab rails and a test weight fitted. It did not enter service. *(AN)*

It has to be repeated that although both these machines were intended for training purposes they formed the bulk of the tank strengths of the Panzer divisions during 1939 and 1940. Although present in reduced numbers, PzKpfw IIs were still major combat components within the Panzer divisions deployed to invade the Soviet Union during 1941. By that time the PzKpfw I had been retired from the combat role but it still soldiered on as a driver-training machine until at least late 1942, as well as in manifestations unforeseen by the original designers.

PzKpfw I

The design of the PzKpfw I, *Sonderkraftfahrzeug 101* (special purpose vehicle – SdKfz 101) was simple, and much influenced by that of the British Carden-Loyd Mark VI tankette, an example of which had been procured from the British company Vickers during 1932. The first examples of the Ausf A off the production lines were at first delivered as unarmed driver training vehicles without a superstructure or turret - they also acted as maintenance training aids. Once the initial driver training machine requirement had been met (15 were produced) production switched to turreted machines having a crew of two and armed with two 7.92mm MG13 machine guns.

To disguise the fact that Germany was manufacturing tanks, and to offer lip service to the terms of the by then moribund Versailles Treaty, both vehicles were given the cover name of *Landwirtschaftliche Schlepper* (agricultural tractor – LaS).

Armoured protection on the PzKpfw I Ausf A (SdKfz 101) was minimal, being just 13mm (0.51in) at the thickest points, rendering the vehicle prone to damage from weapons as light as anti-tank rifles. Another shortcoming was the Krupp petrol engine. As well as providing insufficient power it was also air-cooled. Insufficient consideration was given to how air could circulate around the engine compartment so the hard-worked engines frequently became overheated under anything other than Eastern Front winter conditions. A consistent shortcoming on the Ausf A involved the suspension system modified from the Carden-Loyd original, with the rear idler wheels acting as

ABOVE: The Krupp LKA (*leichte Kampfwagen Ausland*) was built in 1938 for export but never actually sold. It was based on the PzKpfw I Ausf A but so many restrictions were placed on the use of secret technology that only the turret and superstructure front had any resemblance to the original. *(AN)*

extra road wheels. The unforeseen result of this arrangement was that not only did the vehicle start to pitch at speed but it could also shed a track when cornering sharply.

This latter condition was largely corrected on the PzKpfw I Ausf B (SdKfz 101) when the rear idler was raised off the ground and the number of road wheels was increased from four to five on each side. The engine-cooling problem was also addressed on the Ausf B by the installation of a water-cooled Maybach engine producing an output of almost double the horsepower. Production of the Ausf B commenced after about 818 examples of the Ausf A had been delivered, the final Ausf B total being 675. Production was farmed out to several manufacturing centres to give them some experience of manufacturing armoured vehicles. Manufacturers included Daimler-Benz, Krupp-Gruson, MAN and Henschel.

Many of the gremlins inherent in the PzKpfw I models came to light when, quite out of character with the original intentions, examples were sent to Spain during 1937 to participate on the Nationalist side during the Spanish Civil War of 1936-1939. Many German 'volunteers' benefited greatly from the experience gained, experience that was to be put to good use during 1939 and 1940. During these early experiences of combat it soon became apparent that the vehicle's armour protection was inadequate, and the machine gun armament was of little use against opposing armoured vehicles, even when armour-piercing ammunition was involved. The vehicles were completely outclassed by the Soviet T-26B tanks employed by the Republicans.

The Ausf B's water-cooled engine required a slightly longer hull to allow space for the radiator, which in turn needed a new design of engine deck. This new hull was also used for a command version, although the first 15 command tanks were built on the Ausf A hull and a further 25 on a hybrid hull between the two hull types. This command version was the *kleiner Panzerbefehlswagen* (SdKfz 265). It proved to be unsatisfactory in the command role as the fixed superstructure was too cramped while the tank was underpowered. Nevertheless four were used in the Spanish Civil War and the command version remained in service until at least 1941. Another Ausf B variant was an open, turretless driver-training vehicle

Left: The Krupp LKB1 was another unsuccessful prototype this time intended for export to Bulgaria. Like LKB3, an air-cooled Krupp engine was fitted but the vehicle had PzKpfw I Ausf A suspension. *(AN)*

and there were also other turretless versions, with normal upper hulls, for maintenance and for ammunition transport. Details of these and other versions are in the variants chapter.

There was also a PzKpfw I Ausf C, also known as the PzKpfw I nA(nA denoting *neues Art* or new model) or VK6.01 (VK: *vollketten* – fully tracked, 6 tons weight, 1st design). Although bearing the same designation as the little PzKpfw I series the Ausf C was a totally different vehicle. It was heavier due to increased armour, overlapping road wheels, a torsion suspension and an entirely new turret and hull. It was intended to be a fast light reconnaissance vehicle for airborne and colonial formations but only six prototypes and 40 pre-series tanks with different tracks were manufactured by Krauss-Maffei during the second half of 1942. It was armed with a 7.92mm EW141 anti-tank machine gun (the Ausf C was one of only two German vehicles armed with this weapon), and a co-axial 7.92mm MG34. The crew remained at two. One reference states that only two were issued to a combat unit, the rest being retained for training purposes.

Another vehicle totally different from the mainstream series of the PzKpfw I was the PzKpfw I Ausf F or VK18.01. This vehicle can be described as an aberration from the usual German tank doctrines for it was designed to provide supporting machine gun fire for the infantry, in effect adopting the British concept of the infantry tank. For this model the accent was therefore on armoured protection (80mm [3.15in] at the front), the provision of which made a considerable visual difference to the overall appearance and reduced the automotive performance, even though an up-rated engine was installed. Appearances were also changed by the provision of interleaved road wheels, wider tracks to help spread the load (which had risen to over 19,000kg [41,887lb] combat loaded) and a torsion bar suspension. The armament remained at two 7.92mm machine guns, this time MG34s. An initial batch of 30 was manufactured by Krauss-Maffei during 1942 but an order for a further 100 was cancelled. Those built appear to have been little used, although a few did see action on the Eastern Front in 1942 and 1943.

ABOVE: The LKB2 also had the Krupp engine and the longer-type PzKpfw I Ausf B suspension. Like the other LKBs it was intended for export but no sales were made. *(AN)*

RIGHT ABOVE: PzKpfw I Ausf C had a new design of hull, completely different suspension and a new type of turret mounting a 2cm gun. The tracks were fitted with rubber pads similar to those used on German halftracks. *(AN)*

RIGHT: PzKpfw I Ausf F was a heavily-armoured tank for attacking infantry positions. *(AN)*

PzKpfw II

The requirement for what was to become the PzKpfw II was issued in July 1934, the first examples, manufactured by MAN, appearing the following year. The early PzKpfw II models differed in many ways from what would follow, especially the suspension arrangements, while the armour was at first minimal, being the same maximum of 13mm (0.51in) as for the PzKpfw I.

First to appear were the PzKpfw II Ausf (a)/1, Ausf (a)/2 and Ausf (a)/3 (SdKfz 121), all with a crew of three. There were slight differences between these three models but all shared a suspension system with six small road wheels each side, grouped in pairs on bogies with leaf springs, all maintained in position by an external girder rail. The PzKpfw II Ausf b incorporated many detail design changes found necessary on the earlier models but it was only an interim model until the Ausf (c)/1 appeared with a new and more satisfactory form of suspension.

The six road wheels each side were replaced by five larger diameter wheels, each independently mounted on leaf springs, while the number of return rollers each side was increased from three to four. Then came the main production run covering the Ausf A, B and C. The production total of these three basically similar models reached 1,113, production not ceasing until April 1940. All these models were armed by a single 2cm KwK 30 cannon and a co-axial 7.92mm MG34 machine gun, while the armour thicknesses were slightly increased to 14.5mm (0.57in). After September 1939, when the PzKpfw II was rushed into combat service in lieu of anything better, it proved to be vulnerable to even the lightest Polish anti-tank weapons. This shortcoming was partially rectified by the fixing of 20mm armour plates to the hull, turret and superstructure fronts. This gave the rounded, cast nose a squared-off appearance.

By mid-1940 the PzKpfw II series was already obsolescent (at best) but it was maintained in production as a light tank until late 1942. However, it was employed more and more as a light reconnaissance tank as time went on, the role it was originally intended for before the outbreak of war. The final

ABOVE: LKA2 was another Krupp design for the export market, this time with a 2 cm gun. Although the chassis was similar to LKA1, a new, wider super-structure and a larger turret were fitted. *(AN)*

RIGHT ABOVE: PzKpfw II Ausf b and six small wheel suspension. *(AN)*

RIGHT: A PzKpfw II Ausf c, A, B or C in original form with a rounded hull front. The differences between these models are very small making exact identification difficult. *(AN)*

Left: An up-armour kit was designed for the PzKpfw II Ausf A, B and C, adding extra protection to the turret and hull front. This tank also shows the commander's cupola backfitted to these tanks. A stowage box was fitted to the right-hand side of the super-structure. *(AN)*

ABOVE: The PzKpfw II Ausf D had a new type of suspension to allow higher speeds. The Ausf E was very similar but had tracks with rubber pads as used on the PzKpfw I Ausf C (see page 14). *(AN)*

mainstream' model was the PzKpfw II Ausf F from FAMO, on which the armour was up to 35mm (1.38in) thick and the weight had increased from the 8,900 kg (8.75 tons) of the earlier models up to 9,500kg (9.35 tons). By the time the Ausf F appeared the basic chassis was being increasingly employed as the basis for other non-tank variants, one of which, the *Wespe* (Wasp) self-propelled 10.5cm light howitzer, was to remain in production until July 1944.

The PzKpfw II Ausf D and Ausf E appeared before the Ausf F. Produced as light tanks in relatively small numbers only (43 from MAN during 1939), these two models were intended to be fast light reconnaissance and general pursuit vehicles. Although both models retained the PzKpfw II designation the only item they retained in common with the other models was the turret. The entire hull, superstructure and suspension were completely new designs. The new suspension had four large road wheels each side, but the Ausf D used all-steel tracks while the Ausf E had tracks with rubber blocks. In the event the Ausf D and E were deemed to be a needless addition to the German inventory so were withdrawn to be converted into flamethrower tanks or *Panzerjäger* (see under Variants).

Other PzKpfw II variants included the PzKpfw II Ausf G with new type interleaved road wheel and torsion bar suspension. The intention appears to have been to produce a high-performance light reconnaissance tank but only 12 were produced. What happened to them has not been recorded. At least one example was used for trials carrying a 5cm KwK39/1 main gun in an enlarged turret.

Much the same can be said for the PzKpfw II Ausf J, a more heavily armoured light reconnaissance tank with an interleaved road wheel and torsion bar suspension. Just 12 were manufactured during 1942 by MAN before other priorities intruded.

The basic form of the Ausf J, suitably modified for series production, was used for the PzKpfw II nA Ausf H and M. Neither got past the prototype stage although at one time large-scale series production was planned. That project was cancelled in December 1942.

ABOVE: The PzKpfw II Ausf F was built with the squared front to the hull. Note the front plate now extends across the superstructure. *(AN)*

Luchs

The final model in the PzKpfw II series bore little resemblance to any previous models. It was the PzKpfw II Ausf L (SdKfz 123) *Luchs* (Lynx), also known as the *Panzerspähwagen II Luchs*. On this vehicle Ausf M torsion bar suspension was again used, but with interleaved steel disc road wheels. MAN developed the chassis. It was intended that the full production version would be armed with a 5cm KwK39/1 gun but in the interim a 2cm KwK38 cannon was installed along with a coaxial 7.92mm MG34 machine gun. Daimler-Benz was responsible for the turret.

In many ways the *Luchs* was perhaps the most successful of the PzKpfw II series, even if it did bear little resemblance to what had gone before. The crew was increased to four and the maximum road speed was 60km/h (37.3mph). In effect the basic PzKpfw II had been transformed from a simple training vehicle into a fast and effective light reconnaissance vehicle that owed little to what had gone before. Although all development work on the *Luchs* and planned future models ceased during January 1943 the type did enter production during September 1943, by which time other priorities had become more pressing. Only 104 out of the 800 units originally planned were manufactured, none of them with the 5cm gun in a new type of turret.

If the 5cm gun had been installed the vehicle would have become the *Leopard* (Leopard) - prototypes were still under preparation when the project was cancelled during January 1943. In the event the *Leopard* turrets already manufactured well in advance by Daimler-Benz were installed on SdKfz 234/2 *Puma* (Puma) wheeled armoured cars (see Ian Allan Publishing's Military Vehicles in Detail No 2).

By 1942 both the PzKpfw I and PzKpfw II had been withdrawn as light tanks as they were completely outclassed in almost every department. Yet the PzKpfw II had proved in service to be a sound design and so lived on. The PzKpfw I also was used for some years, although in the more mundane form of ammunition supply vehicle conversions and improvised mobile gun mountings.

BOTH PAGES: These four photographs show PzKpfw I C in use for training in France. Thirty-eight had been issued to *Panzer Abteilung 503* of *LVIII Panzerkorps* and were used for training during 1943, but there is no evidence of whether the vehicle was used in combat after the D-Day landings. The colour scheme is overall dark yellow, with no visible markings apart from a German cross on each hull side and white turret numbers.

The photographs appear to have been taken when the PzKpfw I C first arrived if we are to judge by the obvious keen interest of so many officers. The 2cm guns have been removed but the machine guns remain in place, and so does the unusual factory fitting of three smoke mortar tubes on the right-front trackguard. *(TAn)*

ABOVE & LEFT: Driver training tanks converted from obsolete PzKpfw I Ausf A which had been returned to the Krupp factory for major overhaul. The turret and superstructure was removed and a grab rail fitted. No seats were provided for instructors, passengers or trainees. *(TAn)*

RIGHT:
A driver training tank based on the PzKpfw I Ausf B during an exercise to recover another tank, in this case a PzKpfw I Ausf B. The rarely-seen view into the hull shows that since there are no seats for anyone except the driver a large box has been fitted beside his position to give somewhere for an instructor to sit. *(TAn)*

Chapter 2
Description

The PzKpfw I and PzKpfw II were both simple machines with no technological refinements and were not designed as combat vehicles.

Both vehicles stood up to the rigours of service life remarkably well, the basic chassis of the PzKpfw II proving to be sound, reliable and capable of conversion for many combat purposes.

PzKpfw I

The overall layout of the tank had been for the most part established by the time the PzKpfw I appeared. After a series of trial configurations had been tested in many countries the numerous alternatives had largely settled down to what became the norm. In other words, the engine was at the rear and the main fighting compartment was at the centre surmounted by the turret. On the PzKpfw I the driver was also in the main combat compartment while the front of the vehicle housed the transmission components and final drive stages. The engine was joined to the transmission by a drive shaft that passed through the fighting compartment. A similar overall layout was also used for the PzKpfw II and has since been adopted for almost every tank ever built (with a few notable exceptions). While the two German training tanks were not the first to adopt this overall layout, their designers were well aware of technical innovations being adopted elsewhere and responded accordingly.

The armour for the two training tanks presented no manufacturing problems for Friedrich Krupp AG and its subsidiaries for it had been making armoured steel for decades for the Imperial German Navy and for fortifications. It was therefore able to make use of an all-welded structure, including the turret, which involved a modicum of sloped, flat armoured plates. What was so noticeable on the PzKpfw I was that the armour provided was nominal, just 13mm (0.51in) at the front, sides and rear, with only 6mm (0.236in) for the hull top and bottom.

Due mainly to the small overall hull width the superstructure overhung the tracks, thereby providing as much internal space as possible for the crew of two; the commander/gunner and the driver. Even so, space was very limited to the point where there was no space available

ABOVE: The straight front plate and dummy driver's visor indicate that this is a PzKpfw II Ausf F. *(JBn)*

for a two-way radio, only a *FunkSprechGerät 2* (FuSprGer 2) short-range receiver set. In practice nearly all inter-vehicle and other communications were therefore limited to hand signals. It was for this space reason that a command version of the PzKpfw I with a larger superstructure was introduced (see under Variants).

The commander and driver sat almost beside each other so, to accommodate both, the one-man turret had to be located on the right-hand side of the vehicle (looking forward); while the driver sat to the left with a hatch behind for access or escape. Five vision ports were located around the superstructure with a further six for the commander in the turret. As mentioned above, the commander also acted as the gunner controlling the two machine guns mounted side by side in an elevating and depressing gun mantlet. A slightly revised internal mantlet was introduced on the Ausf B. The two machine guns were both air-cooled 7.92mm MG13 that, apart from a few trial installations, were rarely exchanged for the standard German machine gun, the 7.92mm MG34.

The engine on the PzKpfw I Ausf A was the 3,450cc Krupp M305, a noisy four-cylinder, air-cooled petrol engine normally fitted in trucks. It delivered 60hp at 2,500rpm but experience demonstrated that this output was far too low for comfort. In addition, the air-cooled engine suffered from overheating under almost any conditions other than the extreme winter temperatures encountered on the Eastern Front. Exhaust temperatures were so high that personnel contacting the exhaust muffler could receive immediate burns. To alleviate these drawbacks an extra air intake louvre was added to the upper engine deck and two scoops were added at the rear to act as exhaust deflectors, but the overheating problem remained with the Ausf A throughout its service career.

Due to these automotive problems a new engine was selected for the PzKpfw I Ausf B. This was the 3,800cc Maybach NL38TR, six-cylinder, in-line petrol engine and water-cooled with a power output of 100hp at 3,000rpm. This was almost twice the power output of the air-cooled engine, one result being that the maximum speed and operational

PanzerKampfwagen I (PzKpfw I)

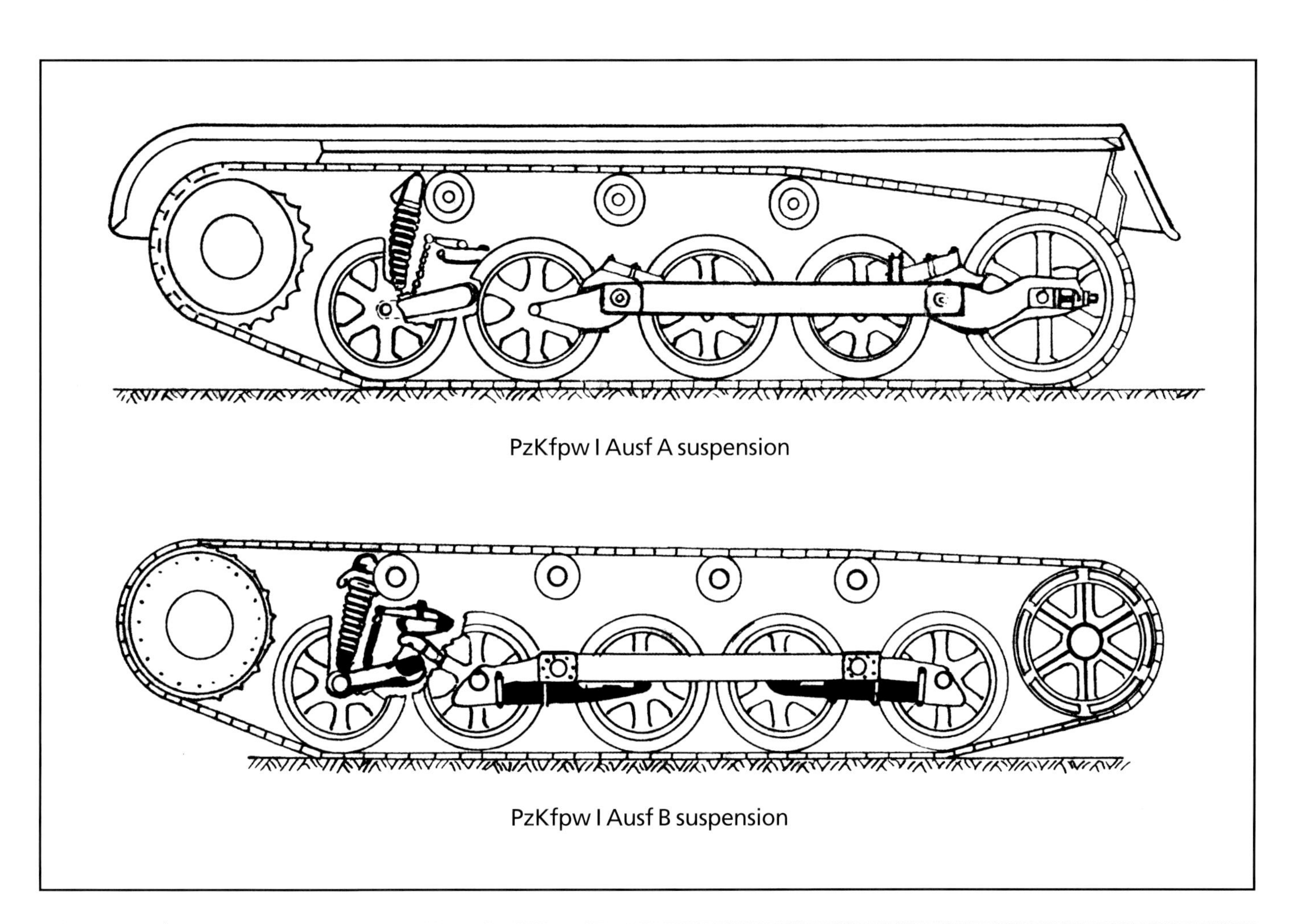

RIGHT: A PzKpfw I Ausf B in pre-World War Two service. *(TAn)*

LEFT: A PzKpfw I *Landungsleger* (demolition charge carrier) in the service of an armoured engineers battalion. *(TM)*

LEFT: A PzKpfw I Ausf B photographed during the Polish campaign, September 1939, and is marked with the all-white crosses used at that time. The right-hand track has broken, allowing a good view of the inside of the sprocket wheel. The front and rear hinged trackguard sections were often removed to help stop the build up of mud, which tended to put the tracks under too much stress so that the pins broke. *(TAn)*

ABOVE: One of the few PzKpfw I Ausf B fitted with a frame aerial for the radio. The mass of stowage hides the turret so it is impossible to tell whether this is a command tank or one of the rare gun tanks fitted with this type of aerial. *(TAn)*

range performances were both improved. Some of the engine compartment air-intake louvres had to be re-arranged (the hull was lengthened slightly) to allow incoming air to flow efficiently through the radiator. A few trial models of the PzKpfw I Ausf A and B were provided with a Krupp M601 air-cooled diesel engine but as it delivered only 45hp at 2,200rpm the project was abandoned.

Both types of engine were coupled by a drive shaft to a sliding pinion gearbox located in the front of the hull. The gearbox had five forward gears and one reverse. It was connected by a cross shaft on each side to the clutch and brake steering units and finally to the drive sprockets. Steering was controlled by hand levers and foot brakes.

The suspension of the PzKpfw I Ausf A consisted of four road wheels each side with the rear idler wheels also in contact with the ground. Front wheel movement was controlled by a coil spring, the rear three wheels and the idler being mounted on bogies with leaf springs and braced by a connecting girder. Three return rollers were also mounted on the hull. Experience demonstrated that this arrangement could cause pitching at speed and was the cause of an unwelcome tendency to shed a track when cornering at speed, so a revised layout was introduced on the PzKpfw I Ausf B. The hull had been lengthened by approximately 400mm (15.75in) to allow airflow through the new-type radiator, so the opportunity was taken to add an extra road wheel and return roller on each side, while the idler wheel at the rear was raised off the ground. The manganese steel track had two guide horns on each 280mm (11in) wide plate.

The restricted internal volume of the fighting compartment and the need to carry 2,250 rounds of 7.92mm ammunition for the machine guns limited the amount of personal kit the crew could carry, but as the vehicle was meant to be a training machine this mattered little at the time of introduction. Various tools and items of recovery equipment, including a towing cable, were stowed around and inside the superstructure. One unusual item on vehicles employed at training establishments was a klaxon horn located on the side of the front hull.

512

LEFT: A PzKpfw II Ausf F in typical markings of the 1941-42 period. The bar under the turret number was used to differentiate between the two Panzer Regiments in a Panzer Division. *(JBn)*

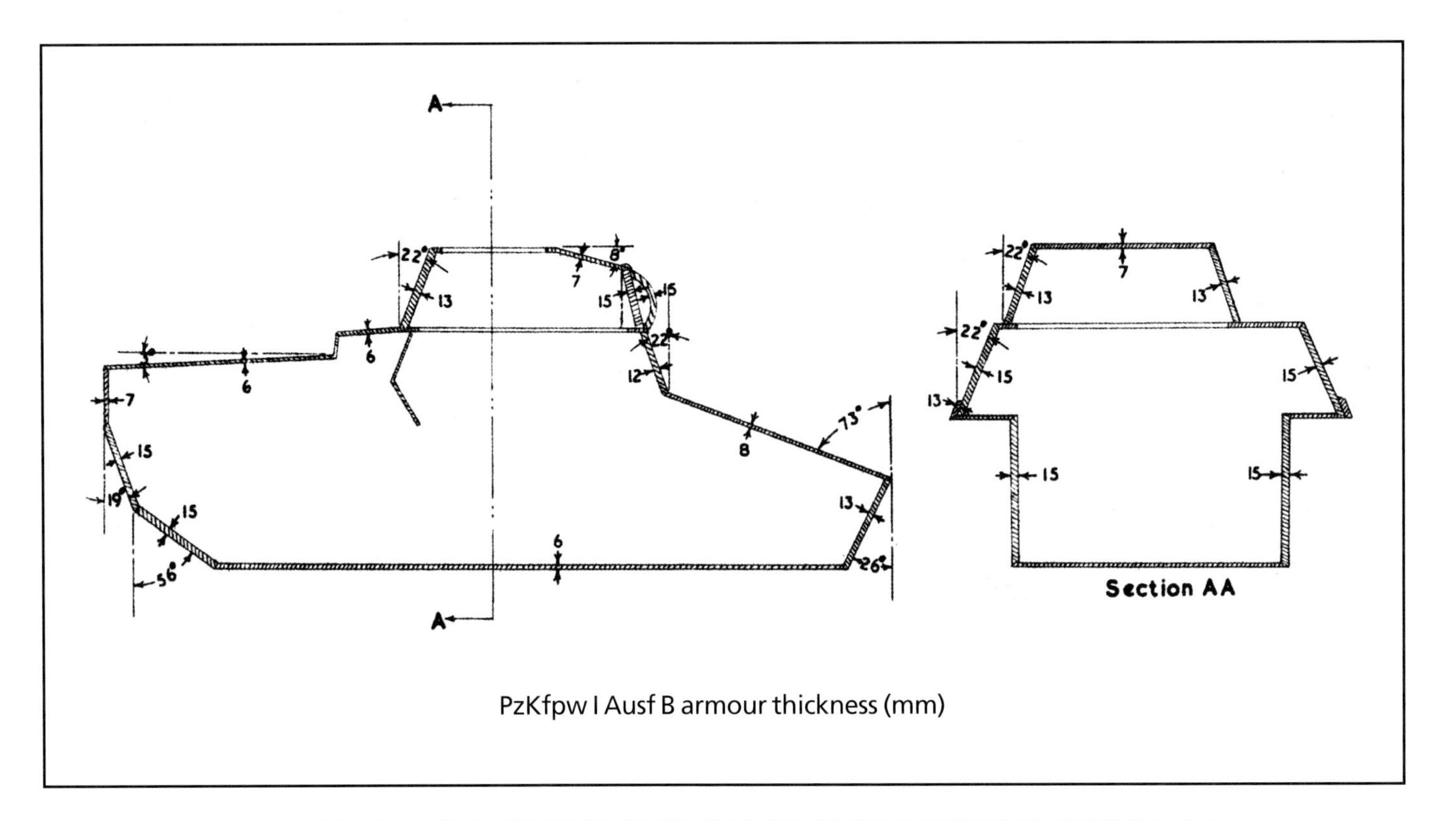

PzKfpw I Ausf B armour thickness (mm)

***PanzerKampfwagen I* (PzKpfw I)**

Model	**Ausf A**	**Ausf B**	**Command**
Crew	two	two	three
Combat weight	5,470kg (12,059lb)	5,800kg (12,786lb)	5,900kg (13,007lb)
Length	4.02m (13.19ft)	4.42m (14.5ft)	4.42m (14.5ft)
Width	2.06m (6.76ft)	2.06m (6.76ft)	2.06m (6.76ft)
Height	1.72m (5.64ft)	1.72m (5.64ft)	1.99m 6.53ft)
Engine	Krupp M305	Maybach NL38TR	Maybach NL38TR
Power output	60hp	100hp	100hp
Speed	37km/h (23mph)	40km/h (24.85mph)	40km/h (24.85mph)
Road range	140km (87 miles)	170km (105.6 miles)	170km (105.6 miles)
Fording	600mm (1.97ft)	600mm (1.97ft)	600mm (1.97ft)
Vertical obstacle	370mm (1.2ft)	370mm (1.2ft)	370mm (1.2ft)
Trench	1.4m (4.6ft)	1.4m (4.6ft)	1.4m (4.6ft)
Armament	two MG13	two MG13	one MG13
Ammunition	2,250 rounds	2,250 rounds	900 rounds

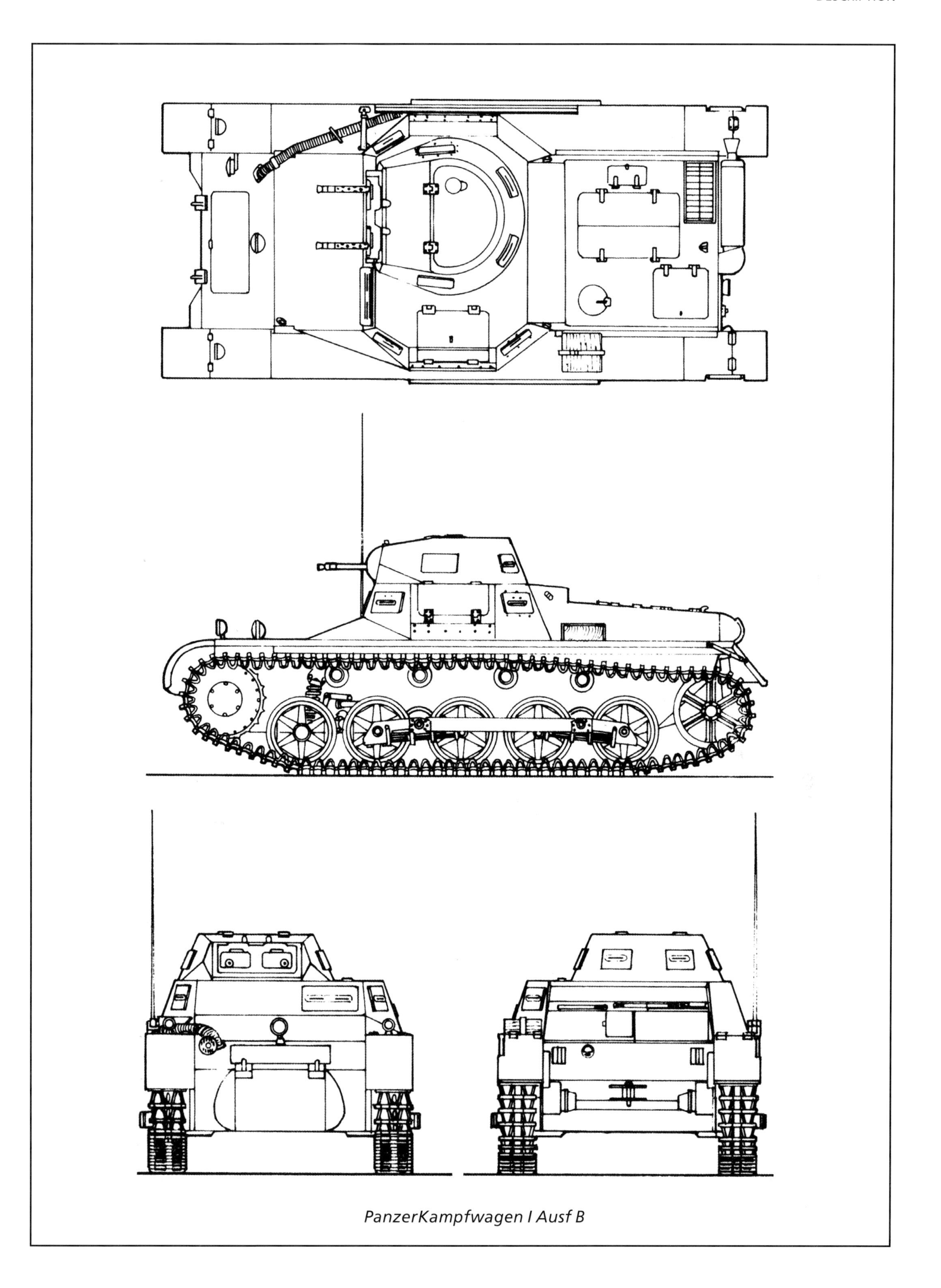

PanzerKampfwagen I Ausf B

LEFT: A fully-equipped PzKpfw I Ausf A undergoing trials on the proving ground. *(TAn)*

RIGHT & BELOW: A PzKpfw I Ausf A with the red and white chequered turret markings used on company commander's tanks before World War Two. Close inspection shows that these are not painted but on a fabric band tied to the turret. *(TAn)*

ABOVE: PzKpfw II and PzKpfw I after combat in Poland, September 1939. The Panzer II displays a painted white bar air-identification mark on the engine deck. *(TAn)*

LEFT: Driver training units were equipped with obsolete tanks. This PzKpfw II is fitted with compressed gas cylinders due to shortages of conventional fuels. *(TAn)*

ABOVE: PzKpfw II in the Norwegian campaign. It is from PzAbt.z.b.V.40 (Panzer detachment 40 for special service). Note, also white-outlined crosses and white-painted 21 on the turret sides and rear. *(JP)*

RIGHT: PzKpfw I Ausf As advance in the Polish campaign, followed by PzKpfw IIs. All are throwing up a great deal of dust from the dry earth. *(TAn)*

I06
I06
I06

LEFT: PzKpfw I Ausf B tanks in the Polish campaign. The leading tank has been fitted with a reinforcing pipe between the idler mounts. The rear tank is from an earlier production run and does not have that feature. Both are painted in the standard grey and brown camouflage scheme of the period. The tactical numbers are painted on trapezoid-shaped plates on the sides and rear of the turrets. The front tank bears white crosses, smeared with mud to make the vehicles less conspicuous. The cursive 'l' on the turret of the front tank is not a scratch on the negative but a personal marking, perhaps the initial of the commander's wife's name. *(JP)*

ABOVE: Swedish Axwall Museum's restored PzKpfw I. The machine guns have been removed. Note the vision block mounting fitted in the vision port. A Klaxon horn is mounted on the inside of the right-hand track cover. *(AxM)*

LEFT: The horizontally mounted radiator fitted in the rear of the hull behind the engine. The air-intake panel is protected by an armoured cover plate. *(AxM)*

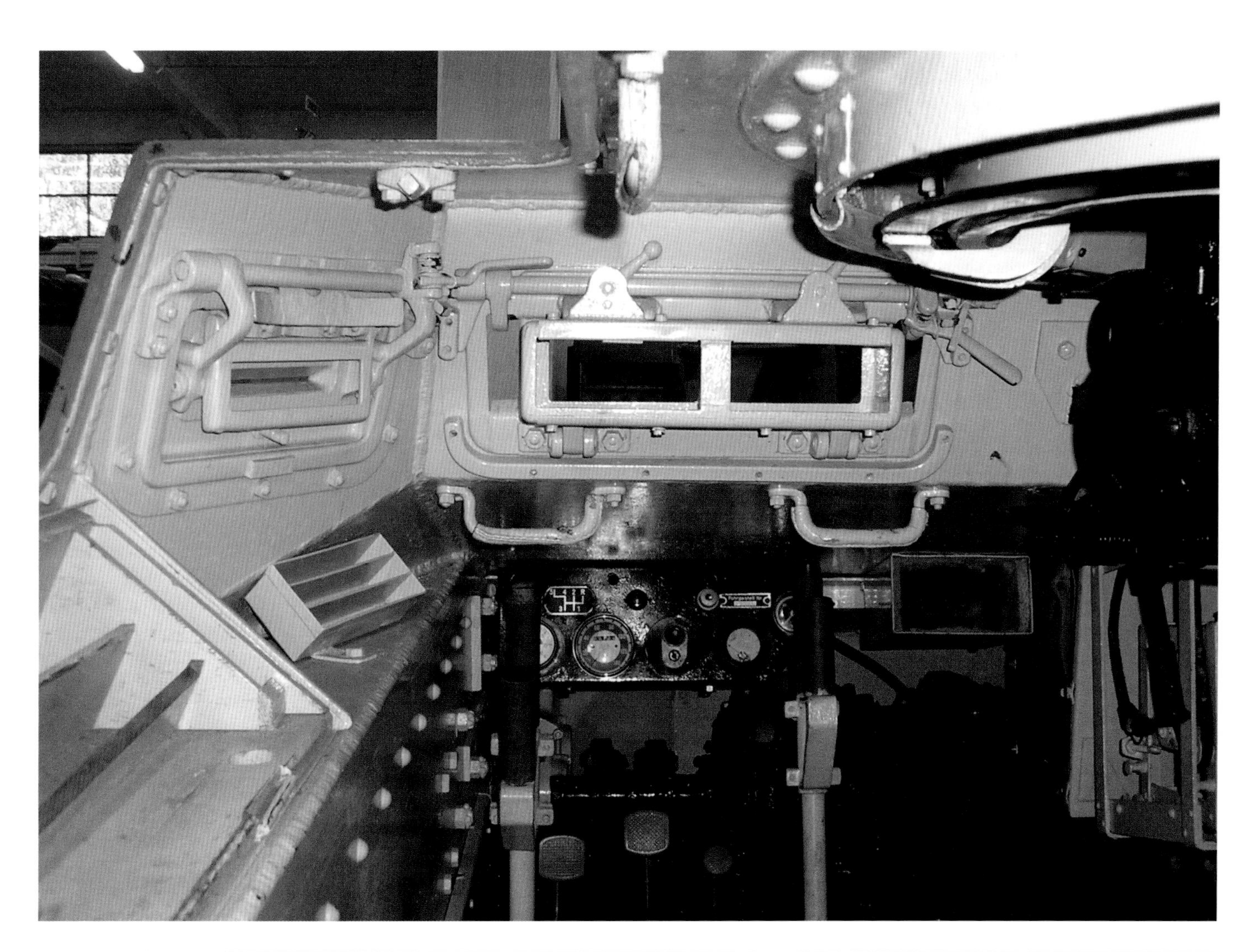

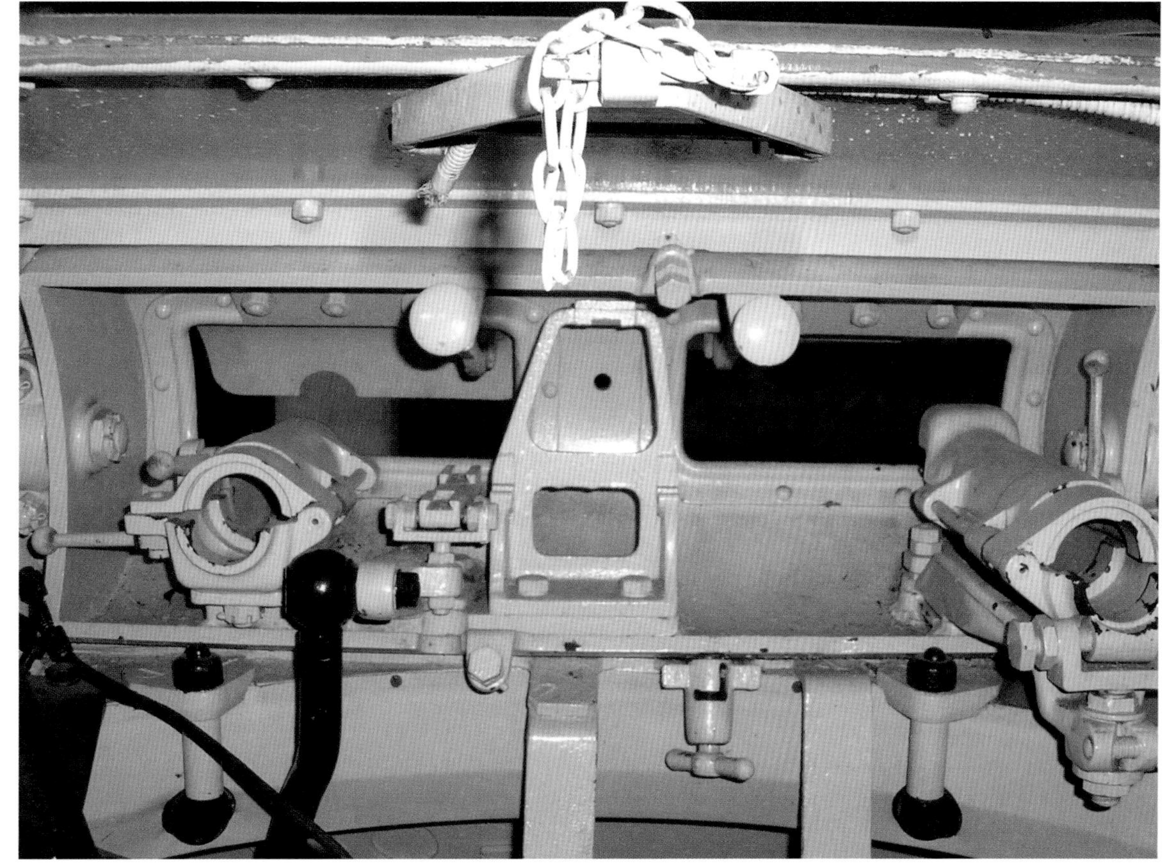

ABOVE: The driver's position in a PzKpfw I Ausf A. To the right of the instrument panel is a small bin to hold the driver's headphones, and to the side is the radio rack. The glass vision blocks are missing but the opening mechanism is visible. *(AxM)*

RIGHT: The turret mountings for the two machine guns. Between them is the mounting for the sighting telescope. The triangular-shaped bracket at the top is the rear support for the sighting telescope. *(AxM)*

ABOVE: The gearbox; note the transverse axles for the roadwheel bogies. Above is the rack for the radio and the mechanism for the pivoting aerial, operated by simply pulling the lever back or pushing it forward. *(AxM)*

LEFT: The turret was traversed manually with fine adjustments being made with this geared unit. *(AxM)*

ABOVE: A PzKpfw II Ausf A, B or C; note the turret number displayed in pre-war and early-war style on a small plate rather than on the turret side. *(AN)*

PzKpfw II

Although the PzKpfw II (SdKfz 121) had the same overall layout as the PzKpfw I it was larger and heavier and fitted with a larger turret. This allowed a heavier calibre main armament to be installed, a 20mm machine cannon together with enough room for a radio operator, positioned in the hull beside the turret, with room to stand up and reload the guns when necessary. In addition, there was also space for a FuSprGer 5 two-way radio with a voice range of approximately 2km (1.24 miles).

Production of the final total of 1,113 of the main PzKpfw II Ausf A to Ausf C series was carried out by several companies, including Daimler-Benz, MAN, Henschel, Wegmann, Alkett, FAMO and MIAG.

The power unit for the main Ausf A to Ausf C production run (and some other models in a slightly modified form) was the petrol-driven 6,200cc Maybach HL62TRM, an in-line, six-cylinder, water-cooled engine delivering 140hp at 2,600rpm. This was connected by the usual drive shaft to a gearbox providing six forward speeds and one reverse. The final drive included reduction gears and a revised driving sprocket compared to the earlier pre-series production machines. There were 96 track links each side although as many as 106 could be installed.

Compared to the earlier pre-series production machines, the suspension was much revised. The earlier small road wheels were replaced by five equally spaced road wheels each side, each on quarter-elliptical leaf springs, and four return rollers.

***PanzerKampfwagen II* (PzKpfw II)**

Model	**Ausf C**	**Ausf F**	***Luchs* (Lynx)**
Crew	three	three	four
Combat weight	8,900kg (19,621lb)	9,500kg (20,944lb)	12,000kg (26,455lb)
Length	4.81m (15.78ft)	4.81m (15.78ft)	4.63m (15.19ft)
Width	2.22m (7.3ft)	2.28m (7.48ft)	2.48m (8.14ft)
Height	2.02m (6.63ft)	2.15m (7.05ft)	2.21m (7.25ft)
Engine	Maybach HL62TR	Maybach HL62TR	Maybach HL66P
Power output	140hp	140hp	180hp
Speed	40km/h (24.85mph)	40km/h (24.85mph)	60km/h (37.3mph)
Road range	190km (118 miles)	190km (118 miles)	260km (161.5 miles)
Fording	800mm (2.62ft)	800mm (2.62ft)	1.4m (4.59ft)
Vertical obstacle	420mm (1.38ft)	420mm (1.38ft)	600mm 1.97ft)
Trench	1.7m (5.58ft)	1.7m (5.56ft)	1.5m (4.92ft)
Armament	one 2cm KwK30 one MG34	one 2cm KwK30 one MG34	one 2cm KwK38 one MG34
Ammunition, 2cm	180 rounds	180 rounds	330 rounds
Ammunition, 7.92mm	1,425 rounds	2,100 rounds	2,250 rounds

However, it was felt that higher speeds would be desirable for the light reconnaissance role so on the PzKpfw II Ausf D and E a totally different suspension was designed. This involved four large-diameter road wheels each side, each on a torsion bar. There were no return rollers. Changes to the hull and superstructure were also introduced but the turret and armament remained as before. Modifications were also made to the drive train, the gearbox was now fitted with seven forward gears. These revised suspension models were manufactured by MAN but only 43 were completed as light reconnaissance tanks before other uses were found for the Ausf D and E (see under Variants). Although these revised vehicles could deliver the required higher speeds, cross-country performance was rated as not as good as with the standard models.

The final mainstream production model of the PzKpfw II mainstream series to be manufactured as a light reconnaissance tank was the Ausf F. On this model the five-wheel sprung suspension was retained while some of the most important drawbacks of the earlier models were at least partially rectified. These drawbacks centred mainly on armoured protection and vision.

The early PzKpfw II models had armoured plates only 14.5mm (0.57in) thick overall (16mm [0.63in] for the gun mantlet). During the 1939 campaign in Poland it was discovered that this protection could be defeated by

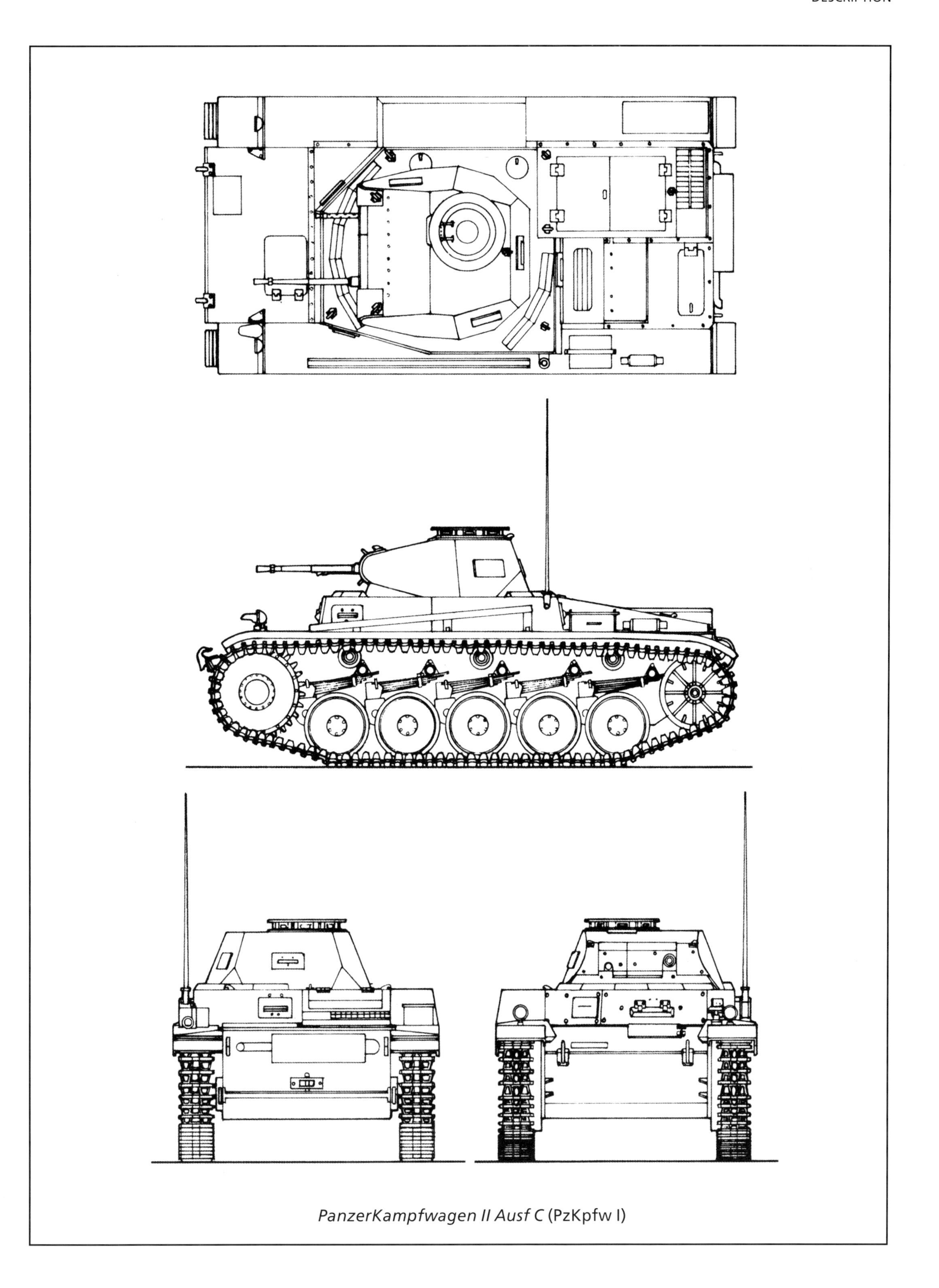

PanzerKampfwagen II Ausf C (PzKpfw I)

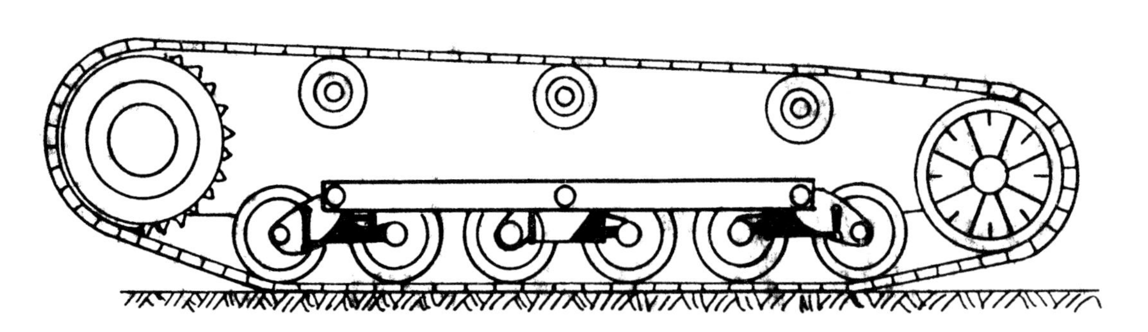

PzKfpw II Ausf a1, a2, and a3 suspension

PzKfpw II Ausf b suspension

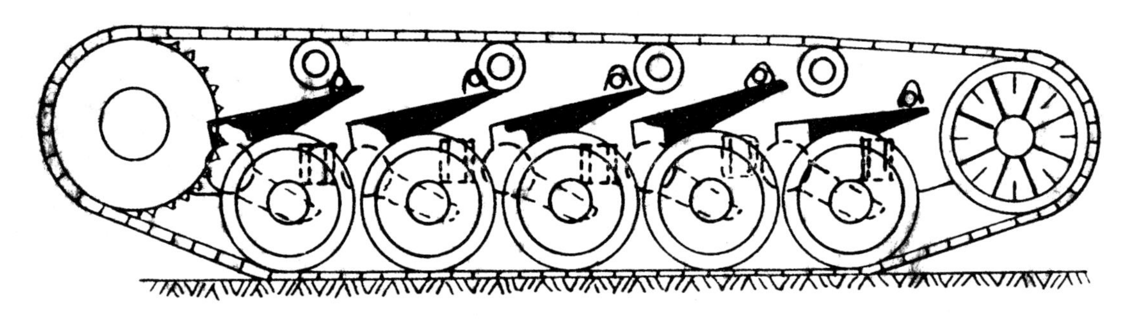

PzKfpw II Ausf c, A, B, C and F suspension

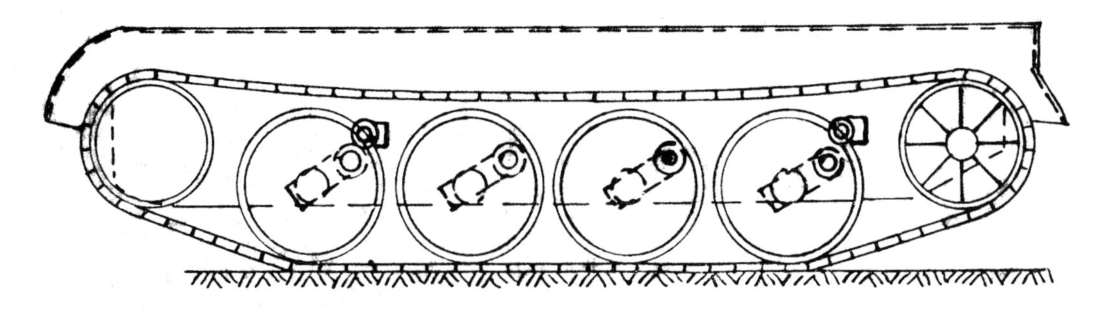

PzKfpw II Ausf D, E and (F) torsion bar suspension

ABOVE: A PzKpfw II during the *Blitzkrieg* on Poland. Note the white crosses are now painted over in yellow. *(BA)*

RIGHT: A PzKpfw II Ausf C during *Barbarossa,* the attack on Russia, 1941. The turret is marked with the symbol for a medical officer – a serpent wrapped around a staff. The numerals and symbol are in red, outlined in white. *(BA)*

ABOVE: A PzKpfw II; note the ready-loaded smoke grenade launchers. *(BA)*

Polish anti-tank rifle fire. By the time the invasion of France commenced, in 1940, extra 20mm (0.787in) armoured plates had been added to the hull, superstructure and turret fronts of the majority of the vehicles scheduled to take part in operations. The original rounded cast hull front was covered and now had a squared-off appearance. On the Ausf F the extra protection was provided by a one-piece 35mm (1.38in) plate on the hull front and 30mm thick for the superstructure and turret fronts. The new hull front shape was almost identical to that of the uparmoured earlier tanks, but the new superstructure front was a single flat plate (the right side was angled back) instead of the split plate of the earlier shape. Also on the Ausf F overall construction was greatly simplified for ease of production.

On the early PzKpfw II models the vision devices were found to be too few and restricted. As an interim measure a retro-fit kit made up of a low cupola with eight episcopes was provided for the commander's position. On the Ausf F a cupola, slightly offset to the right, was fitted as standard.

The commander was seated towards the rear of the turret, under a roof hatch and controlled the armament. The radio operator sat in the hull to the left of the turret, facing rearwards and was provided with a vision port. The driver was seated in the hull to the left of the front, a fact disguised on many vehicles by the provision of a dummy vision slot on the right as an attempt to draw enemy fire away from the driver's position.

Throughout all but the latest models of the PzKpfw II series the main armament was a single 2cm KwK 30 cannon, a close relation to the 2cm FlaK 30 air-defence cannon but fitted with a shorter barrel. This cannon, a Rheinmetall product, was mounted in an internal mantlet co-axially with a single 7.92mm MG34, the MG34 having become the standard German machine gun by the time the PzKpfw II entered

ABOVE: An up-armoured PzKpfw II; note how a spare wheel was carried on the glacis. A tow cable was carried on the original rounded glacis. The markings are for the 2nd Panzer Division, 1940. *(AN)*

production. The cannon was effective against only the most lightly protected opposition while the high-explosive projectile carried too small a payload to be much use against most ground targets. These drawbacks were already apparent by the time the Germans invaded France but production of the PzKpfw II as a light reconnaissance tank was maintained until December 1942. On some late production examples of the PzKpfw II, including the Ausf L, the main cannon became a 2cm KwK38, basically a KwK30 modified by Mauser-Werke AG to increase the cyclic rate of fire.

The later machines

As mentioned in the opening section of this account, the late development models of both the PzKpfw I and II bore little visual or design resemblance to what had gone before. The changes varied from entirely new engines and drive trains to revised hull, superstructure and turret outlines but the main change was to the suspension systems.

Both on the PzKpfw I Ausf C (also known as the PzKpfw I nA) and the PzKpfw II Ausf G, J and L (the Ausf H and M were not produced in quantity) the previous suspensions were replaced by large-diameter interleaved road wheels on a torsion bar suspension. The interleaved road wheels and the revised suspensions gave a smoother ride for the crew while the wheels were easier to manufacture, especially on the high-speed PzKpfw II Ausf L (SdKfz 123) *Luchs* (Lynx) where the road wheels were steel discs (in addition, the revised hull enabled the crew to be increased to four with the addition of a gunner). On the debit side mud and snow tended to become compacted between the wheels when in operation, so that under winter conditions on the Eastern front this mush froze solid and had to be chipped out before the vehicle could move again.

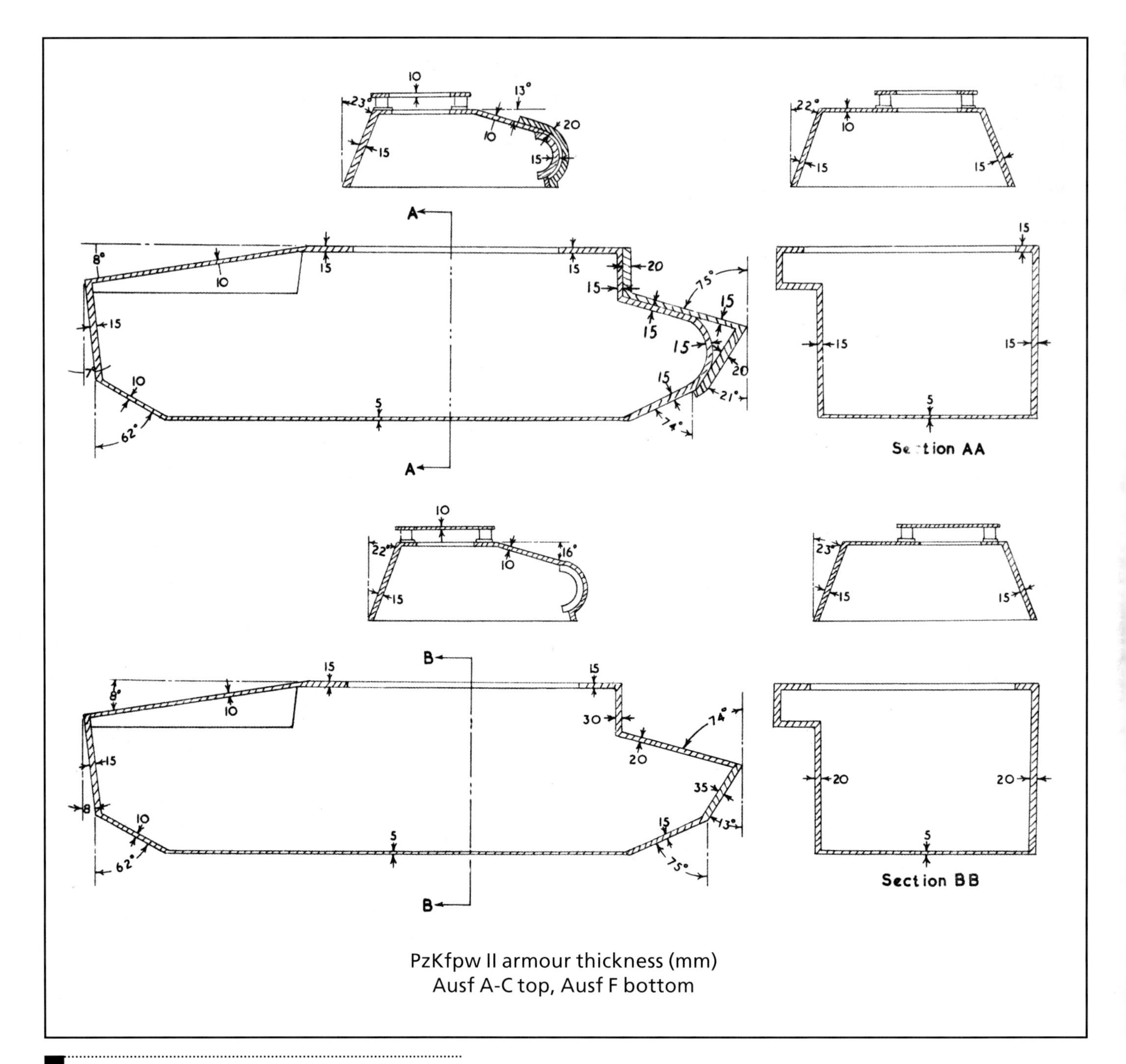

PzKfpw II armour thickness (mm)
Ausf A-C top, Ausf F bottom

Production

PzKpfw I

Pre-war production totals for the PzKpfw I Ausf A, including driver training machines, was carried out between February 1934 and June 1936, the final total reaching 1340.

Pre-war production totals for the PzKpfw I Ausf B, including dedicated training machines, was carried out between July 1936 and November 1938, the final total reaching 841 including 442 driver training tanks. One hundred and forty seven of the latter had armoured hulls to allow conversion into fighting tanks by switching the superstructure and turret from tanks where the chassis was beyond repair, and a number of these conversions did take place.

The total number of *kleinePanzerBefehlswagen* built was 190, including six on the Ausf A chassis. Production was carried out from 1935 to 1937.

War year production and conversion totals were as follows:

	1939	1940	1941	1942
Ausf C	-	-	-	40
Ausf F	-	-	-	30
15cm sIG 33	-	38	-	-
4.7cm PaK 36(t)	-	172	30	-

ABOVE: PzKpfw II Ausf L *Luchs* (Lynx) was a completely new design intended for reconnaissance and was fitted with high-speed suspension. This is one of the prototypes. *(AN)*

PzKpfw II

The initial pre-series models of the PzKpfw II reached a total of 100 between May 1936 and March 1937. Full-scale production of the Ausf A, B and C models commenced during March 1937 until April 1940, by which time a total of 1,113 units had been completed. Production and conversion totals are as follows:

	1939	1940	1941	1942	1943	1944
Ausf C, D and E	15	10	6	282	-	-
Ausf F	-	90	42	23	-	-
Luchs	-	-	-	20	77	7
Marder II	-	-	-	327	204	-
7.62cm PaK 36	-	-	-	184	8	-
15cm sIG 33	-	-	7	5	-	-
Wespe	-	-	-	-	518	144

chapter 3

Armament

The armament of the PzKpfw I and II was light with mounted machine guns. Later this armament was improved by mounting a 20mm cannon.

When the vehicle was under development no other dedicated main armaments were available and there was no space for them, the overall turret dimensions of both vehicles being too small for anything larger without drastic modifications.

Machine Guns

At the time the PzKpfw I was introduced the standard German air-cooled machine gun dated back to 1912. This was the 7.92mm Dreyse, originally a recoil-operated water-cooled machine gun with a noticeably light but reliable construction. As the Imperial German Army had invested heavily in Maxim machine guns the Dreyse never did gain full service acceptance. However, when the *Reichswehr* decided there was a requirement for a light, air-cooled machine gun (in the 1920s) the Dreyse design was extensively reworked at a reasonable cost to rapidly produce an air-cooled weapon, the 7.92mm MG13.

Although the gun did not meet the specifications already prepared by ordnance planners, during 1932 the MG13 was accepted for service as an interim weapon until more suitable designs were completed. The MG13 was really too long and cumbersome for many ground roles but with a shortened barrel it proved to be quite suitable as the armament of the PzKpfw I. Ammunition could be fed from a 75-round saddledrum magazine although for tank use a 25-round box magazine was preferred.

The MG13 had a short German infantry service career for by 1938 most of the type had been sold on the international market, mainly to Portugal, but some were still in service within a few infantry units as late as 1940.

The MG13s of the PzKpfw Is deployed in the Spanish Civil War were useless against other tanks, so a few had turrets rebuilt locally. This involved inserting an armoured 'collar' between the turret body and the roof to allow the mounting of a single Breda 20mm cannon to replace the twin MG13s.

Towards the end of service life a few PzKpfw I tanks had the main armament changed to the 7.92mm MG34. The MG34 entered service

ABOVE: A KlPzBefWg on the Panzer I Ausf B parked between two PzKpfw III gun tanks. The location is France during the *Blitzkrieg* of 1940. *(TAn)*

during 1935 and 1936 and was an advanced Mauser design intended to act as a general-purpose machine gun. It was devised to be a basic gun that could be readily adapted for tripod or bipod mountings, fortification mountings, vehicle installations varying from co-axial to ball mountings, and various other vehicle and air defence applications. Ammunition could be fed from belts holding up to 250 rounds or from 75-round saddle drum magazines.

The MG34 formed the co-axial machine gun armament of the PzKpfw II and all of the early war year German tanks. It proved to be reliable, sturdy and fearfully effective in all its intended roles but it was expensive to manufacture. This led to the development of the 7.92mm MG42 that impinges on this account only as an alternative secondary armament for the *Marder II* and perhaps some 'fortification' turrets. The MG42 was manufactured using as few costly machining operations as possible, much of the construction consisting of sheet steel stampings and spot welds, but it proved to be an even more effective weapon with a high cyclic rate of fire. It utilised 50-round linked belts for the feed and could be installed in as many types of mounting as the MG34, plus a few others.

Model	MG13	MG34	MG42
Calibre	7.92mm (0.312in)	7.92mm (0.312in)	7.92mm (0.312in)
Length	1.341m (52.8in)	1.219m (48in)	1.22m (48in)
Barrel length	720mm (28.3in)	627mm (24.7in)	533mm (21in)
Weight	11kg (24.25lb)	11.1kg (24.5lb)	10.6kg (23.37lb)
Muzzle velocity	823m/sec (2,700ft/sec)	755m/sec (2,477ft/sec)	820m/sec (2,690ft/sec)
Cyclic fire rate	550rpm	900rpm	1,500rpm

ABOVE: A rare front view of the famous PzKpfw I *modificado*, which was converted to mount a 2cm cannon during the Spanish Civil War. *(TAn)*

Cannon

There was only one cannon associated with the PzKpfw II, the 2cm *KampfwagenKanone 30* (2cm KwK 30) (although late production examples, including the *Luchs*, did mount the similar 2cm KwK 38). This recoil-operated cannon was a close relative of the 2cm *FliegerabwehrKanone 30* (2cm FlaK 30) air-defence cannon designed by Rheinmetall-Borsig but with a shorter 50-calibre barrel. Another change to suit the armoured vehicle mounting was that a 10-round box replaced the usual 20-round box magazine of the FlaK model.

Numerous ammunition types could be fired from the KwK30 but fell into two main categories, armour piercing and high explosive, both with or without a tracer element. The armour piercing round weighed 330g (0.73lb) while the high-explosive round weighed 300g (0.66lb). The armour-piercing projectile could penetrate 23mm (0.9in) of armour at 100m (109yd). There was also the rarely obtainable tungsten-cored AP40 armour-piercing projectile that weighed only 140g (0.3lb) the dense core of which penetrated 43mm (1.7in) of armour at 100m (109yd). Maximum effective range of the armour-piercing round was 1,200m (1,312yd) and 2,000m (2,187yd) for the high explosive round.

Calibre	20mm
Barrel length	1.1m (43.3in)
Weight, KwK30	64kg (141.1lb)
Weight, KwK38	58kg (127.8lb)
Muzzle velocity	
armour piercing	780m/sec (2,560ft/sec)
high explosive	880m/sec (2,887ft/sec)
Cyclic fire rate	
KwK30	280rpm
KwK38	450rpm

ABOVE: The 7.62cm PaK 36 gun is being removed from a *Marder* on the PzKpfw II Ausf D chassis. The *Marder* is being carefully driven out from under the servicing gantry that takes the heavy load of the gun. *(TAn)*

The cyclic rate of fire for the KwK30 was 280 rounds per minute (rpm) but due to magazine changing and other factors this was reduced to a practical 120rpm. The reworked KwK38 had a practical cyclic rate of 200rpm.

4.7cm PaK 36(t)

The 4.7cm PaK 36(t) anti-tank gun mounted on the first of the *Panzerjäger*, the *4.7cm PaK 36(t) (Sf) auf PzKpfw I Ausf B*, was originally produced in 1936 by Škoda of Pilsen for the Czechoslovak Army but fell into German hands after they took over Czechoslovakia during 1938. For its time the Czech gun, the Škoda 47mm kanon KPUV vzor 36, originally a towed weapon, was perhaps the most powerful of its type available capable of penetrating 60mm (2.36in) of homogenous armour at 1,200m (1,311yd). It fired an armour-piercing projectile weighing 1.64kg (3.62lb) or a high-explosive shell weighing 1.5kg (3.3lb) from a muzzle-braked barrel of 43.6 calibres. Maximum possible range was 4,000m (4,375yd) and the muzzle velocity was 775m/sec (2.54ft/sec).

German ordnance planners were so impressed with their booty that the production lines at Pilsen were kept in being until 1942. The ammunition facility was still in production in 1943. Production was gradually phased away from the towed version to a fixed pedestal mounting suitable for *Panzerjäger*. On the PzKpfw I example the mounting provided a traverse of 17.5° either side of centre, and an elevation of from –8° to +10°.

ABOVE: The left-hand side of the 4.7cm PaK 36(t) on the cradle and mount used on the *Panzerjäger I*. *(TG)*

7.5cm PaK 40/2

Development work on the 7.5cm PaK 40, designed by Rheinmetall-Borsig at Unterlüss, started during 1939 but it was not until late 1941 before series production could commence on any scale. The gun was an enlarged version of the 5cm PaK 38, a gun soon overtaken by increases in tank armour, and both towed and tank versions were developed.

The demands for *Panzerjäger* carrying such a gun grew to the extent that the PaK 40/2 appeared, basically the towed gun retaining its upper carriage and intended for mounting on a support frame, as on the *Marder II*.

The muzzle-braked gun barrel was a nominal 48 calibres long, delivering a muzzle velocity of 792m/sec (2,598ft/sec). As with other such guns, numerous ammunition types could be fired but again fell within two main categories, armour piercing and high explosive. Two main types of armour-piercing round were available, the standard solid shot or a tungsten-cored projectile, the AP40. While the latter were far more effective than the standard shot the tungsten needed for the dense core became increasingly short in supply due to raw material shortages. This AP40 shot weighed 4.1kg (9lb) and could penetrate 154mm (6.06in) of armour at 500m (546yd). By contrast the standard projectile weighed 6.8kg (15lb) and could penetrate 135mm (5.3in) at the same range. A useful high-explosive shell weighed 5.74kg (12.65lb) and had a maximum range of 7,680m (8,400yd). The maximum effective anti-armour range was 1,800m (1,968yd).

On the *Marder II* the barrel traverse was limited to 32° left and 25°right. Elevation was from –8° to +10°. The gun weight, as installed, was approximately 750kg (1,653lb).

7.62cm PaK 36

The *7.62cm PanzerabwehrKanone 36* (7.62cm PaK 36) was, by 1941, one of the standard Soviet artillery field pieces designated the 76-36 and when captured was rapidly absorbed into the German field artillery inventory as the *7.62cm FeldKanone 296(r)* (Field cannon 296[r]). So many of these guns fell into German hands that it was decided to extend their utility as dedicated anti-tank weapons. For this a muzzle brake was fitted and the chamber was modified so that the original propellant cases could be 'necked' to accommodate modified 7.5cm PaK 40 rounds.

ABOVE: The right-hand side of the 4.7cm PaK 36(t). *(TG)*

A German ammunition production facility was established and kept in being until 1945.

The number of guns converted was 358 during 1942, 168 during 1943 and 33 during 1944. Of these some were destined for the *Panzerjäger* role, including the *Panzer Selbstfahrlafette für 7.62cm PaK 36 auf Fahrgestell PzKpfw II Ausf D* (SdKfz 132). When installed on this vehicle on a modified field carriage the barrel traverse was 25° left and right with the barrel elevation from –5° to +16°.

The 51-calibre barrel of the 7.62cm PaK 36 fired a 7.54kg (16.62lb) projectile that could penetrate 120mm (4.72in) of armour at 500m (547yd). The muzzle velocity was 740m/sec (2,428ft/sec). Also available was a high-explosive shell weighing 6.2kg (13.7lb) with a maximum range of 10,400m (11,374yd). A tungsten-cored AP40 armour piercing round was theoretically available for this gun but it was rarely fired due to tungsten shortages.

15cm sIG 33

So convinced was the *Reichswehr* of the value of artillery deployed by infantry formations that the development by Rheinmetall-Borsig of a 150mm howitzer (actual calibre 149.1mm began as early as 1927. Production of a horse-drawn type did not commence until 1936, with a mechanised traction version soon following. It proved to be so successful that it was one of the few weapons kept in continuous production throughout the war years at both the AEG-Fabriken at Berlin-Henningsdorf and the Böhm Waffenfabrik at Strakonitz.

The *15cm schweres Infanterie Geschütz 33* (15cm sIG 33) was actually a howitzer capable of high-angle fire, despite the designation as a gun. The overall design was very conventional, the barrel being just 11.4 calibres long to produce a maximum range of just 4,700m (5,140yd) with a high-explosive shell weighing 38kg (83.77lb). Maximum muzzle velocity was 240m/sec (787ft/sec).

Creating the *15cm sIG (Sf) auf PzKpfw I Ausf B* consisted of placing the entire howitzer and carriage (including wheels) onto the top of a turretless PzKpfw I, a total weight of around 1,800kg (3,968lb). Once installed the total traverse was limited to that of the field carriage, namely 5.5° either side. Elevation was from –4° to +75°. These same elevation and traverse movements remained the same on the PzKpfw II equivalent.

ABOVE: A *Panzerjäger I* with what appears to be an early version of the unit marking of PzJagAbt 521, without the stag's antlers that usually surround the shield. *(TG)*

LEFT: The breech and mount of the 4.7cm PaK 36(t). Access for the driver was difficult since he had to pass under the mount and around the supporting pillars. A range table has been attached to the inside of the shieldwall. The driver's visors are visible under the mount. *(TG)*

RIGHT: A view from the left into the fighting compartment of a *Panzerjäger I* shows that the curved moving gunshield did not completely protect the crew from shots entering. Daylight can be seen in several places. *(TG)*

Chapter 4
Variants

The success of *Blitzkrieg* operations during 1939 and 1940 also revealed that to carry the Panzer Division concept to a logical end many variants on the basic chassis would be required.

As production of the main combat vehicles could only rarely be interrupted, recourse had to be taken to converting existing vehicles whose combat life was at or approaching an end. Among these latter vehicles were the PzKpfw I and II.

PzKpfw I Command

One of the main reasons for the development of the *kleine Panzerbefehlswagen SdKfz 265* (KlPzBefWg – small armoured command vehicle) was the lack of space inside the PzKpfw I for anything other than a receive-only radio installation. Space for a larger two-way installation could only be provided within a vehicle with a raised fixed superstructure and a further raised cupola for observation purposes. An accordingly modified PzKpfw I was duly produced by Daimler-Benz, the first example appearing during 1935. Access to the interior was via two-piece side hatches. The first six examples were built in 1935 on PzKpfw I Ausf A hulls, with a raised superstructure section the size of the turret. Access to the interior was through the normal hull hatch and the turret hatch that had been moved to the top of the new superstructure. A further 25 were built on modified Ausf A hulls and then 159 on Ausf B hulls, the last in late 1937. All 184 had an improved raised section covering the whole fighting compartment, with access through a two-piece hatch in the left side as well as through the roof hatch.

A few were combat trialled in the Spanish Civil War but performed poorly. Even with the enlarged superstructure the interior remained too cramped to accommodate the vehicles' radio transmitter and receiver installation, map table, observation and survey instruments, a single 7.92mm MG13 ball mounting in the superstructure front (later changed for a MG34 mounting), together with a crew increased to three by the addition of a radio operator to allow the commander to control the tank unit.

While the FuSprGer2 and FuSprGer6 installation was meant to be standard although some models appeared with alternative radio installations, at least one requiring the use of a

ABOVE: A KlPzBefWg on the Panzer I Ausf B chassis in the prewar two-colour camouflage scheme, the grey and brown are clearly seen. The vehicle has not yet been equipped with the backfitted cupola. The salute is being taken by Hitler and Mussolini. *(TAn)*

rigid-frame aerial array. At least three different installations were produced and there may have been others.

For all its faults the KlPzBefWg remained in service until late 1943, mainly because there was usually no suitable replacement. By 1943 some surviving examples had been converted to front-line ambulances although casualty carrying capacity was probably restricted to a single stretcher case. For the ambulance role the machine gun was removed and the ball mounting position plated over.

PzKpfw I Maintenance

Mention has been previously made of the first 15 PzKpfw I examples being delivered purely as open-topped training machines, known as the *PzKpfw I Ausf A ohne Aufbau*. Starting during 1936 there was also a *PzKpfw I Ausf B ohne Aufbau*, another driver and maintenance training machine, at times equipped with charcoal-burning gas generator system to conserve petrol for other purposes.

Eventually some of these vehicles were issued as maintenance and light recovery vehicles (*Instandsetzungskraftwagen I*) to support armoured vehicle formations in the field. Accessible internal space was occupied by items such as batteries, oil containers and as many maintenance and repair tools as could be carried. The basic crew remained at two although up to four fitters often rode on the vehicle perched in whatever positions they could find. The last of these unarmed maintenance and recovery vehicles had been withdrawn by the end of 1941 for they were really too small and light for their tasks.

PzKpfw I Supply

There were two phases to the development of the PzKpfw I ammunition and supply carriers intended to support front-line armoured formations. The first was the *PzKpfw I – Fahrgestell als Munitionsschlepper*, 51 of which were converted from PzKpfw I Ausf A. The conversion involved removing the turret and

LEFT: A KlPzBefWg on Panzer I Ausf B chassis with the first type of backfitted cupola. The raised section behind the fighting compartment is a stowage box and not part of the armour. A unit-made single jerrican rack, one of many variations, holds a single can. *(AN)*

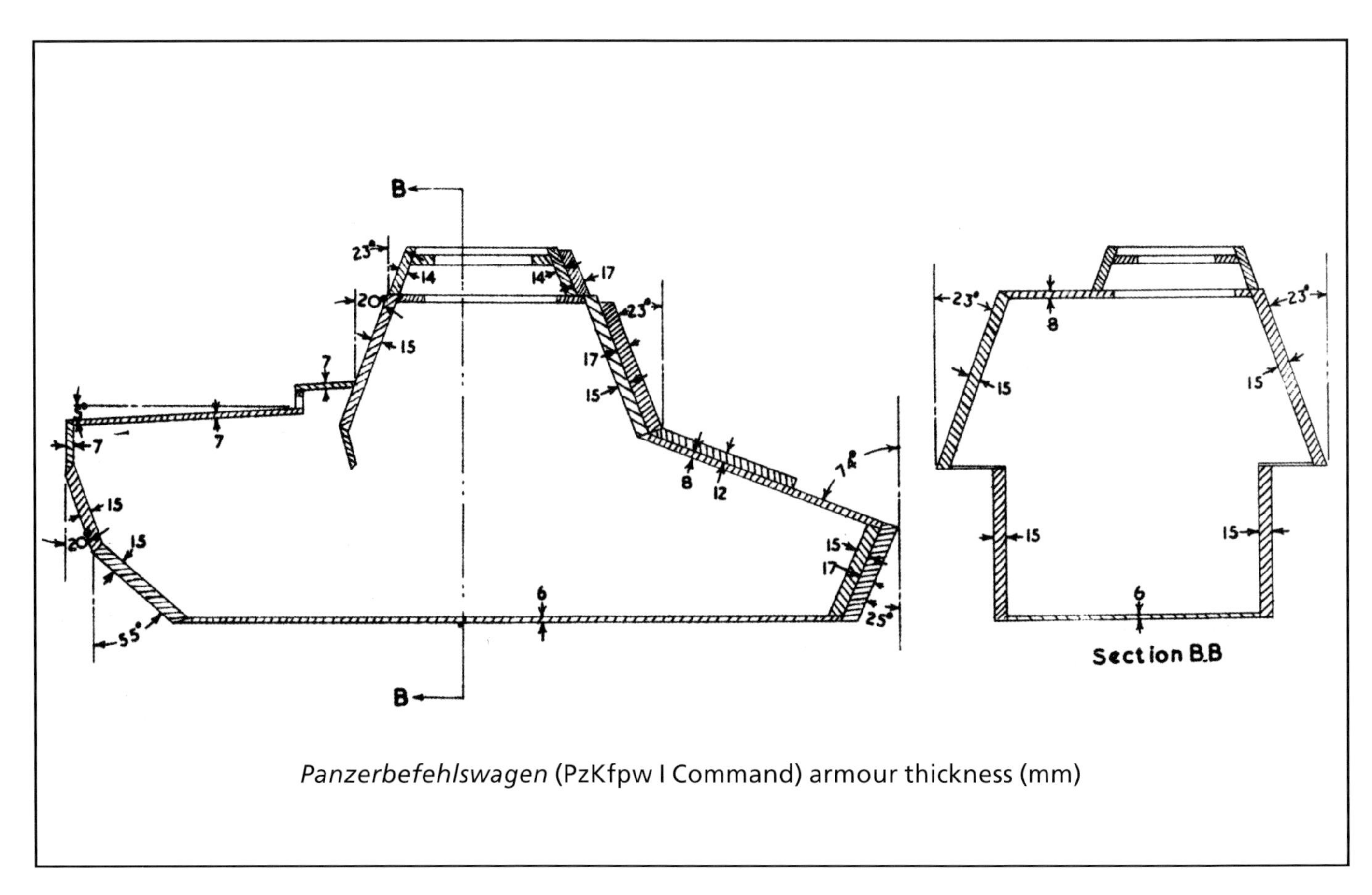

Panzerbefehlswagen (PzKfpw I Command) armour thickness (mm)

Panzerbefehlswagen (PzKfpw I Command)

ABOVE: A KlPzBefWg on the PzKpfw I Ausf B chassis. The most interesting feature is the frame aerial for the radio. This is not only a rarely seen fitting but is a most unusual type with a support at the front for the bent-down section. The gun-mounted PzKpfw I Ausf B behind is even more unusual in having the same type of aerial. Unfortunately the unit and date are not recorded but this is believed to date from exercises held in 1937. *(TAn)*

replacing it with a two-part circular hatch covering the turret ring. Ammunition and/or other supplies were simply carried within the available internal space. The driver was often the only crew member, though a commander was also officially required. No armament or radio equipment was carried.

The second development phase started from early 1942 onwards when withdrawn examples of the PzKpfw I Ausf A and B were also converted to *gepanzerter Munitionsschlepper* (SdKfz III) *auf Fahrgestell PzKpfw I Ausf A und B*, this time by simply removing the turret and replacing it by a large steel box to carry ammunition and/or combat supplies. The original intention to remove the superstructure was usually overlooked. The box could also be covered by a canvas tilt.

Many of the PzKpfw I turrets removed during these and other conversions were released for mounting in fixed fortifications, usually the *Atlantik Wall.* By early 1944 over 500 such turrets had been so installed. Most of these 'fortification' PzKpfw I turrets had the original machine gun armament changed to two 7.92mm MG34s, although in a few cases a mantlet for only one MG34 (or MG42) was installed.

PzKpfw I Infantry Gun

Among the findings from the combat analyses following the 1939 Polish campaign was that armoured formations had to keep their artillery fire support with them wherever they went and that meant replacing the existing horse-towed artillery batteries by self-propelled artillery platforms. Several long-term projects to develop such platforms had started by early 1940 but mechanised infantry units within armoured formations needed something fairly rapidly.

The result was the *15cm schwere Infanterie Geschütz Selbstfahrlafette auf PanzerKampfwagen I Ausf B* , one of the most basic tracked, self-propelled (Sf) artillery platforms ever devised. The turret and the superstructure forward of the engine firewall were removed from a PzKpfw I Ausf B and a frame fitted across the hull. A 15cm sIG33 heavy infantry gun, complete with wheels, trail and gun shield, was then simply mounted on the frame with the wheels fitting into troughs. A high and prominent box-like shield super-structure, open at the top and rear, was built up around

ABOVE: A PzKpfw I *Munitionsschlepper* (munitions carrier) on an Ausf A chassis. The vehicle is passing through ranks of captured Dutch troops, 1940. *(TAn)*

LEFT: A PzKpfw I *Munitionsschlepper* (munitions carrier) in what appears to be factory fresh condition on excercise in Germany. *(TAn)*

ABOVE: The sIG33 PzKpfw II (Sf) self-propelled gun. Although the photograph has been retouched it shows the correct stowage on this side of the vehicle. *(AN)*

the gun. The new steel shield was about 10mm (0.39in) thick and increased vehicle height to 2.8m (9.2ft). There was no other armament or even comforts, such as seating, for the on-board crew of three, while access to the driver's position was difficult. On-board ammunition stowage for the 38kg (83.8lb) projectile was minimal so other vehicles had to be employed as ammunition carriers each carrying the two gun crew members who could not be accommodated with the gun.

These simple conversions were carried out by Alkett at Berlin-Tegel, 38 vehicles being hastily converted during February 1940. The results were therefore ready for the campaigning in Belgium and France during May and June 1940; thereafter they appeared on other fronts. Despite their generally unsatisfactory nature the last unit still equipped with these makeshift measures was not disbanded until mid 1943.

PzKpfw I PaK

The 1940 requirement for self-propelled artillery was matched by a need for self-propelled anti-tank guns. Once again recourse was made to the PzKpfw I Ausf B chassis, this time carrying a commandeered Škoda anti-armour gun known to the Germans as the 4.7cm PaK 36(t): the *tchechoslowakisch* – Czechoslovak origin. These guns were greatly favoured by German ordnance staff as they were more powerful than their own anti-tank weapons in service in 1940, while the suitably modified pedestal-mounted guns could be readily manufactured on the still operating production line at the Skodawerke, Pilsen.

The result was the *4.7cm PaK (t) (Sl) auf PzKpfw I (SdKfz 101) ohne Turm*, later acknowledged to be the first of the German self-propelled anti-tank platforms known as *Panzer-jäger*, or tank hunters. For this adaptation the

ABOVE: A sIG33 PzKpfw II (Sf) during trials in Germany. All 12 built were sent to North Africa so the presence of birch trees shows that despite appearances this is not a combat photograph. *(TAn)*

turret and the entire upper superstructure of a PzKpfw I Ausf B were removed and replaced by a fixed gun shield 14.5mm (0.57in) thick. The top and rear remained open while the two crewmen serving the gun stood on the hull floor each side of the gun. Changes were also made to the air intakes over the engine deck. A commander and the driver completed the crew and stowage was provided to carry 86 rounds of 47mm ammunition.

The conversion work was carried out by Alkett, Berlin with 202 conversions being carried out between March 1940 and February 1941 in two batches; an improved gun shield design was fitted to the second batch. The last examples were not phased out of front-line service until late 1943. (In addition, 200 similar conversions were completed using captured French Renault R-35 light tank chassis.)

It has to be emphasised the *Panzerjäger* were protected and mobile anti-tank gun platforms, not front-line combat vehicles meant to act as tanks. Their role was to either stalk or ambush enemy armour and then retreat as rapidly as possible.

PzKpfw I FlaK

Perhaps the least known of the PzKpfw I conversions was that carrying a 2cm FlaK 38 low-level air-defence cannon. After the adoption of self-propelled artillery and anti-tank gun platforms it was deemed that air-defence guns were also needed and the *FlakPanzer I* duly appeared during early 1941. They were the first of their kind and were converted from *PzKpfw I – Fahrgestell als Munitionsschlepper Ausf A.* It seems that these were converted simply because they were the vehicles used by a supply unit selected for conversion to Flak. Only 24 conversions from well-worn vehicles were made with the work, by some accounts, being carried out by Stöwer of Stettin.

The usual removal of the turret was augmented by the removal of the rear and sides of the hull superstructure. A steel frame then became the platform for the cannon. The cannon was placed on the standard turntable field mounting located slightly to the right-hand side

15cm sIG 33

Model	**15cm sIG 33**	**4.7cm PaK 36(t)**
Crew	four	three or four
Combat weight	8,500kg (18,739lb)	6,400kg (14,110lb)
Length	4.67m (15.32ft)	4.42m (14.5ft)
Width	2.06m (6.76ft)	2.06m (6.76ft)
Height	2.8m (9.2ft)	2.25m (7.38ft)
Engine	Maybach NL38TR	Maybach NL38TR
Power output	100hp	100hp
Speed	40km/h (24.85mph)	40km/h (24.85mph)
Road range	140km (87 miles)	140km (87 miles)
Fording	600mm (1.97ft)	600mm (1.97ft)
Vertical obstacle	370mm (1.2ft)	370mm (1.2ft)
Trench	1.4m (4.59ft)	1.4m (4.59ft)
Armament	one 15cm sIG 33	one 4.7cm PaK 36(t)
Ammunition	four rounds	86 rounds

ABOVE: A 15cm sIG 33 (Sf) auf PzKpfw I Ausf B crossing a broken bridge in the French campaign of 1940. It has been identified elsewhere as gun A of *sIG Kompanie 701*. *(TAn)*

(looking forward) of the platform to allow access to the driver's position inside the hull. The carriage shield was retained but reshaped to suit the front superstructure layout. Fold-down side flaps provided extra working area but the working space proved to be too limited for air defence operations. The full crew, including two drivers, could consist of up to eight personnel so there was quite simply not enough room for them all on the vehicle, especially during moves. Crew kit and equipment had to be towed behind each *Flakpanzer I* in a trailer formed from the cannon's transport carriage fitted with a wooden container. The members of the crew unable to travel on the gun travelled in accompanying support vehicles, basically unarmed carriers based on the PzKpfw I Ausf A with the thinly unarmoured front and sides built up to protect the seating, ammunition and other equipment stowage – the top was open. Each *Flakpanzer I* was served by a few of these support carriers which were converted from captured British Bren Gun carriers.

The *Flakpanzer I* were of limited use as air-defence weapons for the maximum operational ceiling was no more than 2,200m (7,200ft) at the very best and even the practical rate of fire of 220 rounds per minute (rpm) could not overcome the lack of a viable explosive payload for the 20mm projectiles. The cramped nature of the working platform did not assist matters and neither did the generally worn-out state of the vehicles, especially the over-heating and over-worked air-cooled engines. In addition, *Flakpanzer I* units were often mistakenly deployed as ground fire support vehicles for the infantry, a role for which they were poorly suited, so the resultant losses were heavy. The last survivors were lost during the 1943 Stalingrad battles.

PzKpfw I – Other

Other uses than those outlined above were found for withdrawn PzKpfw I, one of the most unlikely being the *Brückenleger auf PzKpfw I Ausf A*. This

RIGHT: A good view into the fighting compartment of a 15cm sIG 33 (Sf) auf PzKpfw I Ausf B. The wheels are being used as a handy place to stow items. A radio set has been fitted to the inside top of the left side armour. The aerial is on the rear of the chassis. *(TAn)*

RIGHT: A vehicle with gun D of *sIG Kompanie 701* on the Russian Front. By now the *Kompanie* (company) had added spare wheel carriers and changed unit markings. The D is barely visible on the bulge for the gun's axle under the white outline cross on the side. The tactical sign for a self-propelled heavy gun company is very clearly visible on the front. *(TAn)*

ABOVE: A 4.7cm PaK (t) auf PzKpfw I. Note how the radio aerial pivoted down into a stowage trough. *(TAn)*

LEFT: 4.7cm PaK (t) auf PzKpfw Is covered with stooks of corn in a field. Although the vehicles' outlines are broken up, this would not be effective camouflage. *(TAn)*

RIGHT: This staged scene shows a 4.7cm PaK (t) auf PzKpfw I with infantry charging against the enemy. A very unlikely operation for an anti-tank gun. *(TAn)*

RIGHT: A 4.7cm Pak (t) auf PzKpfw I in action against a target in a Russian town. *(TAn)*

LEFT: A troop of 4.7cm PaK (t) auf PzKpfw I ready for loading aboard ship. The crews have put everything possible into boxes secured to the vehicles. *(TAn)*

LEFT: One of the above vehicles being lowered into the hold of the ship. The lack of any lifting points meant that hoist cables had to be passed behind the wheels and under the chassis. *(TAn)*

ABOVE: A 4.7cm PaK (t) auf PzKpfw I captured by the British. *(TAn)*

was a bridging vehicle formed by turretless PzKpfw I Ausf A hulls surmounted by short lengths of combat bridging, the intention being that they would be driven in series into dry gaps to allow other vehicles to cross the resultant bridge. The light suspension of the PzKpfw I Ausf A was quite simply too weak to assume the resultant loads but the experience gained during trials was put to use on later bridging vehicles.

Another combat engineering role for the PzKpfw I was as a *Ladungsleger*, literally explosive charge layer, the charge being intended to clear battlefield obstacles. For this role the PzKpfw I, usually an Ausf B that still retained its turret and machine guns, carried a 50kg (110lb) boxed charge that could be emplaced by one of two methods. One was sliding the charge down a ramp fitted over the rear of the vehicle. Another method carried the charge in a thinly-armoured box mounted on two arms that held it above and behind the rear of the vehicle. A cable was pulled from inside the tank to open the bottom of the box and drop the charge. In both cases the carrier vehicle moved a safe distance from the charge before it was detonated under remote control. Exactly how many vehicles were converted for this purpose has not been found recorded, as they appear to have been locally devised field conversions. The number involved was probably limited to approximately 20.

Another PzKpfw I field conversion was carried out in North Africa, this time involving the replacement of the right-hand machine gun in the turret of an Ausf A by a portable infantry *Flammenwerfer 35* (flamethrower 35) with a range of up to 25m (27yd) in approximately one-second bursts. A similar conversion had been carried out on a few PzKpfw I tanks operating during the Spanish Civil War but for either location (Spain or North Africa), the numbers involved were small.

PzKpfw II – Command and Observation

While there were no dedicated PzKpfw II command and observation vehicles, a few 'special purpose' conversions were completed. Most involved some form of frame antenna array for use with various ground-to-ground and ground-to-air communication systems. This included forward area artillery observation and reconnaissance vehicles.

PzKpfw II – Infantry Gun

In general the PzKpfw II underwent the same chain of weapon carrier conversions as for the PzKpfw I. One involved the same *15cm schwere Infanterie Geschütz* (15cm sIG 33 heavy infantry gun) used for the PzKpfw I equivalent, but this time the conversion was far more involved as it was realised that the hasty PzKpfw I conversion was too high at 2.8m (9.2ft). While the gun remained much as before, a new cradle and carriage were provided to suit the fixed open installation that limited the resultant vehicle's overall height to just 1.9m (6.23ft). A trial conversion of a PzKpfw II Ausf B revealed that the gun was too bulky for the chassis so an enlarged hull, still using PzKpfw II components, had to be developed. The end result was heavier, longer and wider than the original light tank to the extent that an extra road wheel was added on each side. The vehicle carried a crew of four and 30 ready-use rounds.

This conversion's designation was *15cm sIG 33 auf Fahrgestell PzKpfw II (Sf)*. Although the design was supposed to be ready for production by Alkett during mid-1941 it was December 1941 before the first of just 12 was delivered, the hold-ups being introduced by prolonged production preparation and unforeseen design-based problems. Eventually further production was cancelled in favour of more pressing priorities. The completed batch of 12 was sent only to North Africa and by early 1943 all had been lost. Six were found dismantled after El Alamein and at least one was rebuilt by the Egyptian Army and used against Israel in 1947.

BELOW: The *Panzer Selbstfahrlafette fur 7.62cm PaK 36 auf Fahrgestell PzKpfw II Ausf D* is often known nowadays as simply the *Marder II D*. The vehicle had a very high silhouette and thin armour, and was only intended as an interim vehicle until better types could be produced. *(TAn)*

ABOVE: Side view of the *Panzer Selbstfahrlafette fur 7.62cm PaK 36 auf Fahrgestell PzKpfw II Ausf D* captured and used for assessment by the British. *(AN)*

RIGHT: A *Marder II D* of 16th Infantry Division. Note the Division emblem in yellow above the white tactical sign for a motorised anti-tank unit. *(TAn)*

ABOVE: A *Marder II* being moved to the battlefront after the first fall of winter snow. *(TAn)*

LEFT: A well-camouflaged *Marder II*, not only covered in branches but also hidden in a gully, a semi-permanent hiding place for the unit. Note the log-lined dugouts in the sides of the gully. *(TAn)*

RIGHT: A *Marder II* in summer. It is painted in a rough pattern of green over the dark yellow base paint. The name 'Marie' has been painted on the driver's visor. A railway loading-gauge table of the vehicles dimensions and weight is on the lefthand front. A unit-made stowage bin has been added to the righthand track-guard. *(TAn)*

PzKpfw II – PaK

The arrival of the tank-hunting *Panzerjäger* has already been noted in relation to the PzKpfw I adapted to carry a Czech-designed 47mm anti-tank gun. Successful as that venture had been, the rapid advances in Allied armour protection meant that something mounting a heavier calibre weapon would soon be needed.

The use of the PzKpfw II chassis to counter heavy armour was one improvised measure amongst many others intended to counter the ever-increasing numbers of Soviet tanks encountered on the Eastern Front. Defeating the armour of the Soviet T-34 and KV-1 tanks called for a high-velocity gun firing a kinetic energy projectile with a calibre of at least 75mm. During late 1941 and early 1942 the only German guns of this nature were the towed 7.5cm PaK 40 and the 7.5 cm KwK 40 version earmarked for the PzKpfw IV series, both only just entering series production by Rheinmetall-Borsig, Unterlüss. At that time the demands for this gun were so pressing that none was available for the self-propelled role, even though German ordnance planners appreciated the need for such a weapon.

The appearance of the Soviet tank hordes meant that the calls for adequately gunned *Panzerjäger* became increasingly strident. As it would take time to develop a dedicated vehicle the way was open for a series of German improvisations to plug the gaps. The calls came at a time when production of the PzKpfw II as a light tank was about to cease so the chassis came under active consideration as a *Panzerjäger* platform. The problem was to find a suitable gun as the Rheinmetall-Borsig guns remained in short supply.

During the early stages of the German invasion of the Soviet Union from June 1941 onwards, masses of Soviet equipment fell into German hands virtually intact. Among the spoils were hundreds of 76.2mm 76-36 field guns. These long-barrelled towed guns already had a good capability as anti-tank weapons but by reconfiguring the chamber and firing modified 7.5cm PaK 40 ammunition the gun could deliver an even better anti-armour performance. Once converted the gun then

Marder III

became the 7.62cm PaK 36, later regarded as being one of the best all-round anti-tank weapons produced between 1939 and 1945. So many of these guns were readily available to the Germans that they were obvious candidates for the *Panzerjäger* role. They were soon combined with the PzKpfw II chassis but in the form of the 'big wheel' Ausf D.

It was decided to convert the Ausf D for its new role as sufficient examples reached the point where extensive overhauls or repairs were needed. Starting during April 1942 a total of 201 battle-worn vehicles were converted by Alkett and Wegmann to accommodate the ex-Soviet guns and become the *Panzer Selbstfahrlafette für 7.62cm PaK 36 auf Fahrgestell PzKpfw II Ausf D (SdKfz 132)*. Much of the original superstructure was retained but once the turrets had been removed the front and side armour was extended upwards to create a combat compartment for the gun crew of three (plus the driver). The top and rear were left open so that the gun and most of its field carriage and shield could be installed. Thirty rounds were carried. This conversion became a considerable success and survivors were not phased out of service until early 1944, by which time another PzKpfw II variant had appeared in the *Panzerjäger* role.

This time it was the PzKpfw II Ausf F with the 'medium wheel' suspension. By the time it was decided that this model could be converted to become a *Panzerjäger* additional examples of the 7.5cm PaK 40 were becoming available so some were suitably adapted for installation in PzKpfw II chassis. In fact supplies of the 7.5cm PaK 40 was so limited during the development and trial period that prototypes were armed with the obsolescent 5cm PaK 38 in lieu of the intended armament.

That was during early 1942 and this time the initial emphasis was on production from new rather than conversions, an economic decision that maintained the established PzKpfw II production lines in being past their intended cut-off point, while at the same time being capable of delivering badly needed *Panzerjäger* with minimal delay. The Ausf F production lines at FAMO, MAN and Daimler-Benz all started to manufacture what was

Model	*Marder II*	*Wespe*
Crew	three	five
Combat weight	10,800kg (23,809lb)	11,000kg (24,250lb)
Length, overall	6.36m (20.87ft)	4.81m (15.78ft)
Width	2.28m (7.48ft)	2.28m (7.48ft)
Height	2.2m (7.22ft)	2.3m (7.46ft)
Engine	Maybach HL62TRM	Maybach HL62TRM
Power output	140hp	140hp
Speed	40km/h (24.85mph)	40km/h (24.85mph)
Road range	190km (118 miles)	190km (118 miles)
Fording	920mm (3ft)	800mm (2.62ft)
Vertical obstacle	420mm (1.38ft)	420mm (1.38ft)
Trench	1.7m (5.58ft)	1.7m (5.56ft)
Armament	one 7.5cm PaK 40/2	one 10.5cm leFH 18M
Ammunition	37 rounds	32 rounds

RIGHT: A quiet country lane with white markings painted on the trees, to aid night vision for drivers. The *Marder II* in the background has had the gun removed and may be in use to carry extra ammunition. *(TAn)*

ABOVE: The flame-thrower *Flamingo*, or PzKpfw II (Flamm). The flame nozzles on each trackguard have been covered as protection against dust. *(TAn)*

still basically the Ausf F hull, drive train and front superstructure but with heightened side and front armour 30mm (1.18in) thick. As with other Panzerjäger the top and rear were left open. A 7.5cm PaK 40/2 was installed on a limited-traverse mounting formed from a steel frame. In many cases a 7.92mm MG34 (a 7.92mm MG42 on a few late production examples) was mounted over the front shield for local and air defence. At least one late-production vehicle was used for trials of infra-red lights and sighting equipment for driving and combat in the dark.

The end product became the *7.5cm PaK 40/2 auf Fahrgestell PzKpfw II (Sf) (SdKfz 131)*, or *Marder II* (Marten II). As with its Soviet-gunned counterpart this variant soon became highly popular and effective so that by June 1943, when production ceased in favour of the *Wespe* (see below), 576 had been delivered. Such was the demand for these vehicles that a further 75 were produced between July 1943 and March 1944 by converting 'retired' examples of PzKpfw II Ausf A, B, C and F light tanks as they were withdrawn from service for overhaul or repairs. By that time most of the work was centred at the Breslau facilities of FAMO. Both 'new' and converted examples of the *Marder II* were still in the front lines when the war ended.

The *Marder II* was supposed to have a crew of three, including the driver, but this was often increased to four. Ammunition stowage for 37 rounds was provided.

ABOVE: A rear view of a *Flamingo* of *Panzer Abteilung (F) 100* in Russia, 1941. The unit emblem of a stylised flame is painted on the rear of the turret. The vehicle number 311 is between the emblems. The large armoured box in the middle of the trackguard contained the flame fuel. Note the smoke mortars. *(AN)*

PzKpfw II – Flamethrower

The ability of flamethrowers to drive personnel out of bunkers and other enclosed areas had been amply demonstrated during World War One so in early 1939 it was decided to produce a tank-based flamethrower system for the same purposes. The vehicle selected was the PzKpfw II Ausf D, the first prototypes being ready by mid 1939 although series production of 90 examples did not commence until May 1940. These were new production vehicles known as the PzKpfw II (Flamm) Ausf A (SdKfz 122), more generally known as the *Flamingo*. Flamethrower vehicles were also built onto Ausf E chassis. Combat weight was approximately 12,000kg (26,455lb).

The flamethrower conversions altered the vehicle's original outline considerably. Two flame projectors were utilised, mounted in small remotely-controlled mini-turrets, one mounted on the front of each trackguard. Each projector could traverse over a 180^0 arc and had a range of approximately 36m (40yd). Sufficient fuel (320 litres [70.4 gallons]) was carried inside the hull for 80 two-to-three-second flame bursts, while four protected tanks containing compressed nitrogen to propel the fuel were located on the hull, two each side. A revised turret mounted a single 7.92mm MG34.

A second production batch of 150 commenced during August 1941 but was terminated after only 65 had been completed. This batch, the PzKpfw II (Flamm) Ausf B,

ABOVE: A captured *Wespe* seen at a collection point. It has no markings, not even the usual German cross. The irregular lump on the hinged back plate is a cover for the gun travel lock. This did not fit completely inside the fighting compartment. *(TG)*

LEFT: A *Wespe* with extra stowage boxes added by the crew together with at least one spare wheel. The tow cable is attached to a towing point in case of need and the MG34 machine gun is mounted ready for action. *(TAn)*

BELOW: Another view of the same captured *Wespe*. Both headlights are in place but the blackout covers are missing. *(TG)*

differed in detail from the first models but proved to be no more successful in the intended role. The vehicle armour was too thin for close-quarter combat on the Eastern Front and many became flaming coffins. The surviving vehicles were withdrawn and used as the basis of *Panzerjäger* carrying the 7.62cm PaK 36 (see above) while the production line also switched to the more urgently needed tank-hunters.

PzKpfw II – Wespe

The most altered of the PzKpfw II variants from the original light tank was the *Wespe* (Wasp), a self-propelled platform for the 10.5cm howitzer that formed the standard equipment of the German light field artillery formations. Numerous makeshift vehicles carrying these howitzers were devised but most proved to be generally unsatisfactory and were retained only because nothing better was to hand.

Something better did appear with the appearance of the *Wespe*, more formally known as the *10.5cm leichte Feld Haubitze 18/2 auf Fahrgestell PzKpfw II (Sf) (SdKfz 124)*. In fact the *Wespe* proved to be so successful in the self-propelled artillery role that the final production total eventually reached 676 howitzer-armed examples, plus a further 159 ammunition supply vehicles below. This was far more than any other PzKpfw II variant. The main production centre was FAMO at Breslau and its subsidiary plant in Warsaw, although Alkett at Berlin-Tegel carried out the design work. Production lasted from February 1943 until July 1944, when the final PzKpfw II-based production run ceased, even though the initial order for the *Wespe* had been for 1,000 units.

To accommodate the bulk of the howitzer on the PzKpfw II required some drastic revision of the basic layout of the late-production Ausf F model. The howitzer had to be mounted towards the rear of the hull so the engine, the same Maybach HL62TR producing 140hp, was moved forward. The hull was lengthened slightly and extra track links (108 each side) were fitted.

LEFT: A heavily retouched photograph from an Allied intelligence report shows a *Wespe* with headlight blackout covers in place. The complicated holder for spare track is noteworthy. *(AN)*

ABOVE: A *Wespe* battery in action on snow-covered ground. The vehicles would have been painted white but most of the paint has worn off. *(TAn)*

LEFT: A *Wespe* ready for action, carrying all the crew's packs as well as the tools for the vehicle. The MG34 machine gun is mounted ready for anti-aircraft fire. The gun letter A is painted on the rear plate. *(TAn)*

Wespe

RIGHT: A battery of *Wespen* loaded on railcars for delivery to the battlefront. *(TAn)*

ABOVE: The Germans carried out experiments to produce swimming tanks. In this one pontoons were attached to both sides of a PzKpfw II. The design was not very successful. *(TAn)*

The number of track return rollers each side was reduced from four to three. Moving the engine forward also necessitated a complete change in the engine air intake louvre arrangements, while the recoil stresses produced by the howitzer meant that the leaf spring suspension had to be strengthened. The combat compartment, open at the top and rear, was protected by sloping plates 18mm thick at the front and 15mm at the sides. The driver had his own compartment forward, next to the transmission.

The howitzer mounted, the 10.5cm leFH 18/2, was a specially developed derivative of the towed 10.5cm leFH 18M, the M (*Mündung-bremse* – muzzle brake) was fitted. The towed version, a Rheinmetall-Borsig AG product manufactured at Düsseldorf, was the standard German light field artillery equipment firing a shell weighing 14.81kg (32.65lb) to a maximum range of 12,325m (13,480yd). Maximum muzzle velocity was 540m/sec (1,771ft/sec). Self-defence was limited to the personal weapons carried by the crew.

The size of the 10.5cm projectiles and charges meant that there was space for only 32 of each on the *Wespe*. Gunners felt that this was too limited a quantity as many fire missions demanded far more firings. To alleviate this drawback the *Munitions-Sf auf Fahrgestell PzKpfw II* was manufactured. It was basically a *Wespe* without the howitzer so that the extra space could be utilised to carry 90 shells and charges held in racks and ready to supply the howitzer-armed vehicles. The slot where the howitzer barrel would normally elevate was closed by a removable plate but the vehicle still had the standard mount for the howitzer. This allowed a munitions carrier to be converted to a fully-equipped *Wespe* by transferring the howitzer from a chassis which, but not the howitzer, had been damaged. The munitions carrier had a crew of three, compared to five for the *Wespe*.

The *Wespe* proved to be reliable, highly efficient and popular in its field artillery context and went on to serve until the war finally ended

ABOVE: Another version of the pontoon was much larger. Shown is the inside of the rear end with the toothed wheels that engaged with the drive sprockets on the tank to power water jet units. *(TAn)*

in May 1945. It also served as a lasting tribute to the sound nature of the basic PzKpfw II.

PzKpfw II – Other

Perhaps the most remarkable of the unforeseen uses for the PzKpfw II series was an amphibious version, the *PzKpfw II mit Schwimmkörper*. The *Schwimmkörper* was a large pontoon with a central opening into which the tank fitted with the tracks protruding underneath. Gebrüder Sachsenberg of Roslau devised the system during 1940, for the amphibious invasion of Southern England that never happened. Once floating, water jet units driven from the main drive sprockets provided forward drive.

While the amphibious concept proved viable, its only use was during 1941 for river crossings on the Eastern Front. For most of their time in the field, only the 18th Panzer Regiment trained and equipped with these flotation devices fought as a normal combat formation.

Retired PzKpfw II chassis frequently became the basis for combat engineer equipment carriers created simply by removing the turrets (which were then diverted to fixed fortifications), plating over the turret opening and either building up a container or a container frame to carry the required equipment. Tarpaulin covers were normally fitted.

A small number of turretless PzKpfw II chassis were also converted to *Bruckenleger* (armoured bridgelayers.) The first of these utilised a one-piece bridge carried over the upper hull and pivoted forward into position using a jib and winch system. This system apparently did not meet with much approval. The bridgelayers that did see service carried two bridge sections sliding horizontally on frames mounted above the hull, the sections being the same as those used individually for the PzKpfw I mobile bridgelayer. The number of vehicles involved in this role was small, probably no more than six, and they do not appear to have been retained after 1940.

BOTH PAGES: A sequence showing the pontoon held up by struts, the PzKpfw II being reversed into the slot, and the successful water trials. The marking WA PrUf 6 / III h on the pontoon indicates the trials are under the direction of *Waffen Prüfungs 6*, the weapons testing division of the *Wehrmacht*. *(TAn)*

ABOVE: PzKfpw I Ausf A tanks from the 3rd or 4th production batch. Note, the vision port on the right rear of the superstructure is not fitted. The vehicles are finished in the original colour scheme of earth yellow, green and brown. The markings carried were designed for the 1937 general exercises, light grey (not white) rectangles with identification symbols. The white-painted M on the leading tank is noteworthy. *(JP)*